MIND OVER MONEY

How to Banish Your Financial Headaches and Achieve Moneysanity

MIND OVER MONEY

How to Banish Your Financial Headaches and Achieve Moneysanity

Dr. Norm Forman

**1987
Doubleday Canada Limited,
Toronto, Ontario
Doubleday & Company Inc.,
Garden City, New York**

Copyright © 1987 by Norm Forman
All rights reserved
First edition

Typesetting by Compeer Typographic Services Limited
Cover design by Don Fernley
Printed and bound in Canada by Friesen Printers

Canadian Cataloguing in Publication Data
Forman, N. (Norm)
  Mind over money

ISBN 0-385-25104-1

1. Money - Psychological aspects.   2. Finance, Personal.   I. Title.

RC569.5M66F67 1987   155.9'2   C86-094929-X

Contents

Introduction	ix
1 The Psychology of Money	1

Part I The Money Complex:
Symptoms of Monetary Headaches

2 The Miser's Misery	13
3 The Spendthrift Syndrome	23
4 The Tycoon's Trauma	34
5 The Bargainer's Bug	43
6 The Gambler's Grippe	51

Part II The Green Therapies:
Banishing Monetary Headaches

7 Cognitive Behavior Therapy	63
8 Destressing and Systematic Relaxation	71
9 Psychodynamics	76
10 Assertive Behavior Training	81
11 Psychological Flashcards	86
12 Letting Go	92
13 Thought Stopping	97
14 Mini Green Therapies	101

Part III Money Stress of Everyday Life

15 The Stress of Budgeting and Life Planning	109
16 Savings and The Unconscious	125
17 Paying Your Insurance Dues	140
18 Where There's Not a Will, There's a Nightmare	152
19 Taxes: Peace of Mind Despite the Inevitable	162

20 Taking Stock of Yourself and Your Investments **172**
21 Credit Cards, Credit Ratings, and Your Fantasy Life **193**
22 Living Within Your Means Even if You Have to Borrow to Do So **203**
23 Going for the Gold in the Golden Years **220**

Part IV Prognosis of Your Monetary Health
24 Achieving Moneysanity **235**

Suggested Reading **245**
Index **247**

To Alyssa, Christine, Gideon, and Jessica—all of whom play a significant role in helping me remember the true priorities of life.

Acknowledgements

I would like to thank the following people for their assistance: David Ball, Alex Di Mauro, Michael Globe, Sam Hastings, Mary Kershaw, Bob Lavers, Debbi Lockie, Shlomo Maital, Dr. Donald Payne, Chris Robinson, Alan Sandler, Ivan Scott, A. D. H. Smith, Jay Smith, and David West. Honorable mention goes to three people whose contributions were significant to this book-journey: Jennifer Glossop, for her expertise and therapeutic approach to the manuscript as well as the author; Larry Hoffman, for his consistently upbeat and positive attitude from the moment I first guardedly told him about my idea for the book; and Rick Palidwor, for his good humor, constant energy, and on-going loyalty in helping me to complete the manuscript. My special thanks go to Chris Snyder for his thoughtful input concerning financial matters.

Introduction

Examining people's psyches has to be one of the most fascinating jobs in the world. Those who do it for a living have examined virtually every human activity, from sexual practices to ax murders, without qualms or hesitation. Only one subject makes them and their clients reticent: money. When it is mentioned, the reference is usually to fees—how much and when they will be paid.

To find out why this was so, I first looked at my own life. I poked, probed, tapped and dissected my memories, thoughts, and reflections like some kind of psycho-surgeon looking for something left behind in a procedure. I discovered that every time I located a money association it was linked up with a significant point in my life, one that had been buried for a long time. Bringing these episodes to the surface taught me a lot, and I soon began to apply what I had learned to helping my clients.

To be fully involved in the game of life, you have to play with a full deck; but when it comes to money, many of us don't. We fail to understand how our attitudes and actions can limit our effectiveness. And yet money, more than almost any other symbol, has shaped our consciousness, and has been a powerful influence on our personality development and our personal relationships.

Because money is so common to our experience, we tend to overlook its psychological effects. All of us "create" money in our own image and use it to satisfy a variety of needs. If the uses are neurotic ones, we end up with monetary headaches. To rid ourselves of our cranial pain, we must become aware of what we are doing and why.

In this book I explore how psychological money problems originate. In Part I, I discuss the major psychological styles and the different hangups we have about our cash. I look at what prevents us from being free to spend, invest, and deal with money. I examine what factors interfere with our enjoyment of money, why we deny ourselves and feel guilty or anxious when dealing with or asking for money, and what emotional needs have been affected by our learning. I explain the factors that are involved in preventing us from making fruitful investments, planning for our futures, and maximizing the funds we have.

In Part II, I introduce the Green Therapies, such as Psychological Flashcards, Thought Stopping, Destressing and Systematic Relaxation, Letting Go, and Psychodynamics, which I have used successfully with my clients. By learning how to understand their problems better, these clients improved their money handling. You can, too.

After that, in Part III, I examine the psychological aspects of such areas as budgeting, savings, taxes, borrowing and credit, estate planning, and related topics. After you have attained some Moneysanity in these important areas, you'll be able to handle your financial life more effectively with the help of the money-management tips at the end of each chapter.

How To Use This Book

At the beginning of chapters 2 to 6 in Part I, there are Moneyanalysis Quizzes. At the conclusion of each chapter is a summary profile and a list of recommended Green Therapies, which are described in chapters 7 to 14 in Part II. The Moneyanalysis Quizzes will help you diagnose your money headaches, and the Green Therapies will help you find the cure. Part III looks at the psychological money stresses of your everyday life: budgeting, saving money, buying insurance, writing a will, paying your taxes, investing, using credit cards, borrowing money, and planning for retirement. If you have problems in any of these areas, you will be directed to the appropriate Green Therapies, which will lead you to Moneysanity Payoffs.

In Part IV, in addition to a discussion of Moneysanity, you will find a chart to help you match your psychological and financial profiles and choose the investment strategies best suited to your money style.

Introduction

By combining your increased financial self-knowledge with concrete money tips, you will be able to improve your attitude to money and at the same time benefit financially. As a result, you might find that you have more money around, and that you get more enjoyment and satisfaction out of it. That's what *Mind Over Money* is all about.

Being liberated in this way means you are free to pursue your muse wherever it takes you, whether it is in the direction of Hermes, the god of profits, or toward a dynamic, lifelong fiscal-management program that will enable you to enjoy the money you have. Either way, you will be able to follow your monetary leanings with security and confidence.

To protect the anonymity of my clients, whom I describe in the case histories, I have changed their names and altered the details of their daily lives.

Chapter 1
The Psychology of Money

I don't know about you, but no one ever taught me the value of a dollar. I don't mean neat little maxims like "A penny saved is a penny earned." I'm talking about the basics of money: what it is, what you can and cannot do with it, and what you can and cannot expect of it. It took me many years to define the role of money in my life and to discover that a philosophy of money is part of a larger philosophy of life.

Many people acquire mistaken beliefs and distorted ideas about finances as they grow up. Later, their early misconceptions interfere with sound money management, and these people turn out to be money neurotics.

Money Neurotics

Of all the neuroses around, the money neurosis is probably the most widespread. Like any neurotic process, it involves unresolved conflicts that are associated with fear and anxiety, and that lead to maladaptive and self-defeating behavior. For example, a money neurotic with an exaggerated fear of being taken advantage of in cash matters might hoard his funds in order to protect himself against an anticipated threat. Another troubled money handler might fly into a rage if her demands for money were not met.

People who are obsessed with money may also be money neurotics. Some are addicted to money and need to have it around all the time. Others look for the highs they get from having a large bankroll in their pockets. And still others have an irrational desire to acquire endless sums of money. Occasional bouts of these symptoms do not make a person a neurotic. Only those people with intense and long-standing symptoms are true money neurotics.

Cash Defined

Money has been defined as anything that passes from hand to hand in payment for commodities and services and is regularly taken with the intention of offering it in payment to others. More simply, it is anything people agree to accept in exchange for things they sell or work they do. The medium of exchange can be anything from animal teeth, shells, beads, and cattle to liquor and cigarettes.

Money also has a personal psychological meaning. It has become a shortcut abstract symbol that stands for the value of things we wish to obtain. Dollar bills in themselves are neutral and uninvolved, but we tend to see beyond them into our fantasies. We get caught up in the alchemical process that transforms cash into objects and services.

Money is man's most clever and creative invention. In all our experience, it is only money that means all things to all people. We think money, like the Greek god Proteus, has the power to assume different shapes at will and can therefore satisfy every need, wish, desire, or fantasy. We attribute all kinds of magical properties to money, and eventually we believe it can do anything; we forget that it is an invention. The fault lies with us, and not with our bank notes.

Money has a way of bringing out the irrational in us. It seems to crawl down to the most remote levels of our personalities and release avarice, jealousy, resentment, and fear. People bearing psychological money scars have lost their connection with the original purpose and use of bank notes.

Learning About Money

How do people get so confused about money matters without even knowing it? Where does this all get started? Like every other self-respecting problem, it begins where you begin—in childhood. Most of us get our distorted attitudes about finances from our parents. Negative, incomplete, and false notions concerning monetary issues are handed down to children who then grow up with distorted views, which they pass on to their offspring. In addition to parents, siblings, close relatives, and good friends may also influence a person's monetary views.

The Influence of Money on Our Lives

There are few love-hate relationships stronger than the one many people have with money. Some of us want it around all the time; a small number shun it as an evil. People often do strange and illogical things with and for their money. Money has helped destroy marriages, friendships, and families, and has contributed to their well-being. To many people, money remains a mystery, understood only by the initiated "high priests" of finance: accountants, stockbrokers, financial planners, and financiers. Money is often seen as a means to achieve psychological security in a world of constant change and turmoil. People think that what is missing most in their lives is an inexhaustible source of funds. Instead, what they really need is an increased sense of security and love, a boost in self-esteem, and a strengthened sense of self-respect.

Monetary Headaches

In one sense, this book is about those things money can't do and the monetary headaches people develop as a result. Money can't buy emotions, such as love and affection, personal states of mind, like inner peace, self-esteem, and contentment, or social attributes, like power, status, or security. People fail when they try to "cashify" these sentiments. Money can never do for us the emotional jobs we have to do for ourselves. A person who feels essentially insecure and unsure of himself, for example, cannot rid himself of these feelings by using money to buy status and self-confidence. For all the trappings of social standing that he buys, he will remain uncertain of his own worth until he deals with the reasons for his insecurity.

Looking for Help

In searching for money rationality, many people read financial books, magazines, newsletters, and money reports. In addition, they take courses, seminars, and classes of all kinds to increase their personal wealth and money-management skills. While these people may learn a lot about financial matters, only a fraction of them will ever go on to practice what they learned. Why does this happen?

It happens because most people's money-earning fantasies are out of sync with their psychological traits and personalities. They are unaware that they themselves prevent their own financial accomplishments and success.

It is easy to read a book or to attend a lecture about investments, about ways of increasing your income, or about monetary risk taking and adventurous buying and selling. But if you are unaware of your money neuroses and how they undermine and sabotage your behavior, you will be unable to take full advantage of what you have learned. You will remain blocked from within. Self-destructive habits will impede you, and you will not feel free to make the most of your money-making skills or manage your money in the best way.

Achieving Moneysanity

A variety of faulty money-dealing styles deeply influences our lives and results in psychological liabilities. Based on my professional work with clients, I know that if you are prepared to explore your personal views about money and to acknowledge the neurotic, self-defeating elements involved, you can become more effective in mastering your financial life. This is what Moneysanity is all about.

The management of money is really the management of the self. To manage yourself—and thereby your money—more effectively, you need to understand your personal psychology of money: what it means to you, your goals in pursuing it, and your attitudes and views about it.

There are neurotic and non-neurotic ways of relating to your money. The object of this book is to assist you to achieve Moneysanity by helping you move from a state of money as "inner tormentor" (headache) to money as "inner mentor" (Moneysanity). Money neurotics tend to value their money for *what it represents* (power, love, superiority, status); whereas people who are psychologically free with money value it for *what it can do* (buy goods and services).

It is not always easy to tell which acts are neurotic and which are not. You could, for example, try to make a lot of money either for what it represents or for what it can do. Planning a well-managed financial future for the security it brings to you and your family is an appropriate (non-neurotic) act, whereas compulsively investing vast sums and finding personal reassurance only in the Dow Jones average is an unhealthy and ultimately unsatisfying act.

The Equations of Money

For many people, money has become one side of an emotional equation; without their realizing it, money has come to equal love, self-worth, freedom, power, or security.

Money = Love

A person who has experienced a lack of affection and care may seek to make up for these deficits by "buying" love—by giving expensive gifts or by purchasing the semblance of affection from a prostitute or gigolo. The money itself frequently gets mixed up in these psychological equations.

This equation (money = love) usually indicates that the person has uncertainties and self-doubts about her abilities to love and be loved. She has learned not to expect love and approval on her own merits. As a result, she feels compelled to use money or its derivatives (gifts, influence, resources) to make herself feel loved and lovable. By her "generosity," she attempts to increase her worth in the eyes of others and at the same time to prevent them from rejecting her.

The same person might also become an inveterate bargain hunter who, in effect, culls favor and "affection" as she asks for special attention and treatment. Similarly, the compulsive shopper buys aggressively to gain a feeling of "love," even if it's only through the artificial exercise of obtaining things. Just as a person who has learned to equate food with love will overeat, so the person who equates money with love will overspend.

Money = Self-Worth

Money often gets confused in people's minds with self-worth, with the need to feel important. Inside, the individual may feel inadequate, as if he doesn't measure up. By purchasing, with money, the external appearance of worthwhileness, he attempts (unsuccessfully) to create the corresponding feelings on the inside. The person in this situation tries to make himself feel better by the equation "money = self-worth." In one form or other, in big or small ways, he tries to compensate for feelings of inadequacy and insignificance by wheeling and dealing, living high on the hog, and generally distributing his finances in ways that quell his inner doubts. He always fails in these efforts.

Money = Freedom

To avoid feeling dependent and passive, people sometimes amass large sums of money. Having enough money will, they believe, keep them from ever having to ask another for help. Here, money is equated with independence, but the freedom this money gives only goes skin deep.

This kind of person feels the need to have money so that she can avoid being controlled or dominated by others. The adolescent who saves enough money to leave home, to get away from the demands of her parents, is a prototype. The fear of being placed in an inferior position—to an employer, spouse, friend, parent—is intolerable to a person who uses this money equation.

Money = Power

One of the most common money equations—money = power—is used by people who attempt to gain control over the lives of others, to get their demands met, and to show who's boss.

This equation allows a person to repress his feelings of helplessness and impotence. He uses money to offset any form of domination by others and to show others he cannot be pushed around. If he feels his power threatened (that is, if there is a chance he will lose it or his money), he will fight tooth and nail to hold on to it. Obsessive money-makers often are driven by power motivations; they use money to show their superiority.

Money = Security

The person who lives by this equation uses money to bring about a feeling of safety. She feels anxious and threatened if she doesn't have money stored away to offset these troublesome feelings. The only thing she seems to be able to rely on consistently is her store of funds, and she will hold on to it and guard it jealously for this reason. When it comes to money, she tends not to trust others and is therefore likely to be miserly with her money. She acts as if she could fend off her insecurity by concentrating on her money and how it can protect her from any dangers. Loss of money would put her in a state of terror and panic.

Money and Loss

The loss of any amount of money upsets most of us and at times even makes us depressed. There are many theories to explain why we get so attached to legal tender. Psychiatrist James Knight tells us: "In the deeper layers of the mind, money, like all other possessions, assumes the role of parts of the body one could lose or, after the fantasy that they have been lost, wishes to regain."

Psychoanalysts say that people accumulate money to protect themselves from loss. They also relate the loss of money to the loss of body parts. The Freudians call this fear "castration anxiety."

Psychoanalysts also believe that it is during the second and third years of childhood (the so-called "anal stage" of development) that the personality patterns develop that will influence our views toward money. According to this outlook the child sees his waste products as precious possessions. Later they become symbolic of all kinds of possessions and eventually of money itself. The analysts say that people who grow up preoccupied with the anal stage of development are likely to be stingy, orderly, obstinate, and overly clean.

Whether or not we agree with these theories, it is clear that our identities become deeply involved with loss, and particularly with monetary loss, whether it's through theft, the depreciation of stocks, or the result of ill-conceived investments.

If we lose our money, we also lose some of our fantasies. For many people, their fantasy life is tied to their sense of well-being. They refuse to give up their fantasies even when it's in their best financial interest to let go.

Why is it so hard for some people to accept loss? Why do we find it difficult to cut our losses and let go when it's in our best interest to do so?

Loss causes a shock to our system. Our emotions are in chaos and we undergo mental suffering. As well, we feel saddened by the sense of having been separated from something very dear to us. Feelings of anger, guilt, and confusion frequently accompany the loss, and we sometimes end up blaming ourselves or others for the circumstances that led to the loss. We may not consciously feel all these emotions but many of them are at work behind the scenes.

When faced with significant financial losses, many of us may at first deny the reality as a way of overcoming the anxiety. People have a similar reaction when someone close to them dies. After some time, we fall into the stage of anger and depression.

At these times, people often feel like failures or "losers." Defeatist feelings may set in and they may worry about the consequences of their losses. Their behavior during these moments may be exaggerated and extreme.

Money loss is a model for all loss and disappointment in our lives, because our hopes, wishes, and fantasies for a better life are tied up with the powerful symbol of finances. Lost money may represent lost opportunities, lost love, lost feelings of accomplishment, or loss of recognition.

If we study how we reacted to these losses in the past, and acknowledge that our responses were self-defeating, we can do better in handling our current money accounts.

Test Your Moneysanity

1. Do you find yourself worrying about the spending, using, or giving of money all the time?
2. Are you inhibited about talking to others about money, particularly about your income?
3. Do you buy things you don't really need because they are great bargains?
4. Do you lie awake at night trying to figure out a way to spend less money and save more, even though you are already saving money?
5. Do you hold on to or hoard your money?
6. Do you regularly exceed the spending limit on your credit card?
7. Does gambling make you feel a burst of excitement?
8. Would you walk blocks out of your way to save a bus fare you could easily afford?
9. Are you constantly puzzled about where your money goes or why there is none left at the end of each month?
10. Do you use money to control or manipulate others?
11. Do you refuse to take money seriously?
12. Do you resent having to pay the full price for any item when you shop?
13. Do you often gamble and spend large sums on your bets?
14. Do you spend a large proportion of your free time shopping?

15. When you ask for money, are you flooded with guilt or anxiety?
16. Are you increasingly anxious about whether you can pay your bills each month?
17. Do you spend money on others but have problems spending it on yourself?
18. Do you buy things when you feel anxious, bored, upset, depressed, or angry?
19. Are you reluctant to learn about practical money matters?
20. Do you think about your finances all the time?

If you're nodding your head in response to even two or three of these questions, you probably have some money headaches. Some people have terrible pounding money headaches that can affect their whole lives, others have smaller, but still nagging, pains that ache from time to time. If the answer to any of these questions is an emphatic yes, *all the time*, put everything else away and read this book right now. If you answered, "Yes, but not always," you might find the ideas in *Mind Over Money* useful in warding off the next attack of a money headache. If you answered, "Never!"—congratulations. Give this book to a friend who does have money headaches and be supportive when he or she tries out the suggestions here.

PART I
The Money Complex: Symptoms of Monetary Headaches

Money headaches come in varying degrees of seriousness. The more severe varieties include such well-known "migraines" as the Miser's Misery, which causes constriction of the financial vessels; the Spendthrift Syndrome, which manifests itself in a loss of voluntary control of the purse strings; and the Tycoon's Trauma, which causes dollar-bill signs on the brain. Two other major fiscal infirmities are the Bargainer's Bug, which causes the victim to constantly try to lower the money pressure, and the Gambler's Grippe, which creates abrasions of the will.

Chapter 2
The Miser's Misery

Moneyanalysis Quiz One:
How Eligible Are You To Be A Miser?

For each question, check the statement that most accurately describes your behavior. Upon completion, add up your score and refer to the explanation at the end of the test.

1. *My thoughts about money tend to drift to*
   a. how I'm going to pay for my basic needs.
   b. a pretty strong concern about being taken advantage of.
   c. how I can hold on to my money.
   d. saving more money.
2. *One of my greatest pleasures with money is*
   a. saving it all the time. I really hate to spend any of it.
   b. fully enjoying what I earn by spending within my budget.
   c. spending it but trying not to go crazy with it.
   d. spending it a little at a time so it will last longer.
3. *If I won a million dollars in the lottery,*
   a. I'd spend a couple of thousand and put the rest in the bank until I got old.
   b. I'd spend a lot of it on all the things I've always wanted and bank the rest.
   c. I'd put the money in the bank and immediately get the best financial help I could, to preserve the principal and make it grow.
   d. I'd put all of it away in the bank and not touch a nickel of it.
4. *When I go shopping for something I need,*
   a. it takes me a little while to get into the spirit of buying.
   b. I go right away and spend money on what I need.
   c. I put it off as long as possible. I can't afford it.
   d. I wait until it's absolutely necessary and spend as little as possible.
5. *Whenever I'm with people, particularly those with more*

money than I have, and the topic turns to finance,
   a. I listen attentively and share my opinions and personal experiences freely.
   b. I listen but don't say much.
   c. I feel a little uncomfortable at first, but then I begin to discuss my views and personal finances.
   d. I remain quiet and get a sense of security from thinking about the money I have and how I plan to keep it for myself.

6. *When I discover I could have bought something elsewhere for less and saved money,*
   a. I make a mental note to check more carefully next time. Then I enjoy my purchase.
   b. I tell a friend about it.
   c. I feel foolish and don't tell anybody about it. I don't think about it for very long.
   d. I get quite down on myself for a long time. I also feel as if I've been tricked.

7. *If a good friend were to ask how much money I have in the bank,*
   a. I would be extremely uncomfortable and feel resentful about the invasion of my privacy. I would not answer the question, even though I know the amount to the penny.
   b. I'd be a little surprised, but I would discuss the topic for a while and then probably tell my friend the answer in very general terms.
   c. I'd ask my friend why she wanted to know, but I wouldn't answer even though I knew the exact amount.
   d. I'd probably smile, give my friend a close round figure, and ask her a similar question.

8. *When my child asks me for an addition to his allowance,*
   a. I listen and tell him I'll let him know. I don't like giving him additional money. I might give it occasionally.
   b. I point out that the object of money is to save it and not to spend it, except for the bare necessities. It makes me anxious to think of how much things cost. I rarely will give it.
   c. I discuss with him how he's been spending what he has. If the request is reasonable, I'll give him some additional money.
   d. I would give it quite freely if it was a relatively

small sum. If it was larger, I'd give it according to how much it fit into our family's budget.

9. *I would be happier*
   a. if I could spend my money more freely and get more satisfaction from it.
   b. if my family didn't press me to buy new clothes or other items. The ones I have can last for a long time.
   c. if I didn't have to spend any of my hard-earned money. I am afraid that one day I might not have any.
   d. if I had more time and more money to spend on myself and my family. I enjoy spending money.

10. *When I go out with people for dinner,*
    a. I occasionally figure out what portion of the bill I owe. Other times I'm more relaxed about it.
    b. I always pay only my part of the bill. I'm keeping a tight rein on my money.
    c. I pay my share most of the time. That's basically the way I like to do it.
    d. I just chip in the amount we all agree on.

Scoring Moneyanalysis Quiz One: Miser

Scoring Key

1. a. 3 points
   b. 0 points
   c. 1 point
   d. 2 points
2. a. 0 points
   b. 3 points
   c. 2 points
   d. 1 point
3. a. 1 point
   b. 2 points
   c. 3 points
   d. 0 points
4. a. 2 points
   b. 3 points
   c. 0 points
   d. 1 point
5. a. 3 points
   b. 1 point
   c. 2 points
   d. 0 points
6. a. 3 points
   b. 2 points
   c. 1 point
   d. 0 points
7. a. 0 points
   b. 2 points
   c. 1 point
   d. 3 points
8. a. 1 point
   b. 0 points
   c. 2 points
   d. 3 points
9. a. 2 points
   b. 1 point
   c. 0 points
   d. 3 points
10. a. 2 points
    b. 0 points
    c. 1 point
    d. 3 points

23–30 points
Whatever other money quirks you may have, niggardliness does not seem to be one of them. You appear to be relatively free of the major symptoms of the miser's headache.

15–22 points
If your score is closer to 22, you probably are pretty good at avoiding compulsive underspending. If you scored closer to 15, however, you may want to diminish some minor inclinations toward miserliness.

8–14 points
There's a good chance that you are somewhat stingy. You may not feel comfortable about your money dealings in general, and could certainly use some help in loosening up.

0–7 points
You have strong symptoms of the miser. The problem is probably deeply set and can be corrected only with personal insight and strong motivation. Read this chapter thoroughly: you are *very* eligible to be a miser.

The words *miser* and *misery* come from the same Latin derivation meaning wretched—an accurate description of the lives of those afflicted with the miser's migraine.

A Case History: Gerald Tightwad

Alice and Gerald know very well how much your head can hurt when it's stuffed mostly with dollar bills. They came to see me because money problems were wrecking their marriage. Gerald is a hospital administrator and Alice is a teacher. They have a five-year-old son.

Gerald has a simple, straightforward monetary philosophy: get a hundred and twenty-five cents out of every dollar. If Alice wants to go sailing or take flying lessons, that's fine with Gerald as long as she uses her own money. Gerald reviews the household balance sheet with a fine-tooth comb every month, and he's content only if there's money left over to put into a savings account.

He thinks about money all the time and worries that others are going to take advantage of him. His main reason for making money is to sock it away. He gets little or no enjoyment from it, and is reluctant to spend it. There's no way he's going to spend "all that money" on a new color TV—the old black-and-white one is fine, thank you.

Alice is an overly patient, self-sacrificing, childlike woman who wears her self-denial on her sleeve. She wakes up every day with a money hangover. No matter how hard she tries to manage the family's financial affairs, she fails miserably in Gerald's eyes. No matter how many times she has told Gerald she cannot pay all the bills and balance the books on five hundred dollars a month, he remains adamant that she must do so. She has come to doubt herself more and more. She is chronically uptight, and she has the bitten fingernails to prove it.

Alice can't stand living this way, and she's told Gerald so every week for the past ten years. He doesn't believe her, partly because she continues to wash his clothes and iron his shirts, clean the house, and look after her own expenses, just as always.

Gerald has the classic miser's headache. The symptoms include obsessional absorption with money, compulsive money hoarding, exaggerated fear of losing funds or being taken advantage of, and a constant inability to enjoy many of the real benefits of money.

An Extreme Case

There are people who go to their graves never enjoying the money they never spent; these people still have the first nickel they ever earned. In its most extreme form, the problem of miserliness can be quite tragic.

A powerful example was the well-publicized case of the postal worker who died in his two-and-a-half room apartment in one of the poorer sections of New York City. An unmarried man, he had worked for the post office for more than forty years and had had a perfect work record. When the authorities examined his cluttered domicile, they were shocked to find a number of envelopes stuffed with twenty-, fifty-, and hundred-dollar bills. In addition, approximately forty thousand dollars was found in a drawer, with bank-account books that collectively totaled two hundred thousand dollars! It was clear that this unfortunate man had died having spent almost none of his hard-earned money.

Understanding the Miser

Like other neuroses, money neurosis begins in childhood. For example, Gerald Tightwad's parents' warped views of money had seriously inhibited the healthy growth and development of his own. As a child, he had felt weak and dependent. By denying money to others, he made himself feel stronger, more powerful, and safer. Having a full piggy bank made him feel more comfortable.

In the process of counseling, Gerald began to understand that his extreme stinginess was based on unconscious feelings of weakness and passivity developed in early childhood. Holding on to his money had become the way he protected himself against the anxiety that arose from feelings of weakness. When this became clear, he was able to let go and become a bit more relaxed about money matters.

Gerald Tightwad's emotional needs caused him to give money a distorted meaning. He had tied his sense of security to his monetary resources. By piling the dollars into a gigantic bankroll, he hoped to create an adult security blanket. But this "investment" didn't work. He still felt vulnerable. The ploy of moving away from people and toward money does not allay the miser's problems. Instead, it leads to poor social relationships and emotional isolation.

Help for the Miser

To be helped, Gerald needed to make three basic changes.
- He had to learn to bring about a relaxed state of mind.
- He had to recognize and challenge his false or mistaken beliefs.
- He had to risk making changes and practice behaving differently.

Relaxation

Relaxation is important because it can be used to displace the arch-enemy of inner peace—pervasive anxiety. The mainstay of Gerald's money affliction was his ever-present, free-floating anxiety. When he felt very apprehensive, he tried to ease the dreadful feelings by increasing his miserly behavior. He neurotically believed that he would feel better only if he kept his money. He was mistaken.

What Gerald needed first was a tool to prevent the buildup of anxiety. I taught him exercises in progressive relaxation—the process of systematically contracting and relaxing body-muscle groups from the feet to the head. Whenever Gerald felt himself getting anxious, he would immediately close his eyes and call forth the inner relaxed state he had practiced achieving.

Challenging False Beliefs

The second thing we worked on were Gerald's misperceptions. For example, Gerald had an abnormal fear that others were going to take advantage of him financially all the time. He felt, for example, that his friend Joe was always trying to get him to spend money on things.

I advised him to keep a notebook in which he wrote down the times he felt others were trying to take financial advantage of him. To help him be accurate in his descriptions I told him to practice his relaxation exercises when he felt stressed.

Gerald reviewed his notes regularly and learned to challenge his irrational perceptions. Soon he saw, among other things, that Joe was not trying to take advantage of him. Later, he was better able to see similar situations in a more rational way.

Making Changes

After challenging his idea about others taking monetary advantage of him, and gradually altering his perceptions, Gerald was encouraged to free up his spending. He opened an "anti-miser" bank account, into which he put money to be spent. He could use it however he liked, but he had to spend it. He also used the Green Therapies to challenge and eliminate the inner commands that told him to be tight with his money.

At first he felt awkward and ill at ease, but eventually he found he could enjoy his purchases. He bought a camera for himself, which he had wanted for years, and for Alice he purchased a bicycle, which she had been longing for.

Gerald was able to correct his money neurosis, but not everybody can. Chronic inability to spend, or miserliness, is often a stubborn problem that is very resistant to change.

Famous Penny-Pinchers

Gerald is not alone in his obsession. A number of well-known people were infamous misers. There is an amusing story about Nathan Rothschild, the financier who lived in London in the early nineteenth century. On one occasion, after taking a hackney cab, Mr. Rothschild gave the driver a very modest tip. The driver maintained his decorum but commented that Mr. Rothchild's daughter Julie gave him much larger tips. The financier retorted that that was okay for her because she had a very rich father.

The famous comedian W. C. Fields was morbidly afraid of being cheated of his money. (Ironically, one of Fields's movies was entitled *You Can't Cheat an Honest Man*.) In a pathological attempt to prevent such an occurrence, he opened approximately two hundred different bank accounts all over the world—each one under a fictitious name.

Fields managed to keep his family and friends away from his cash not only while he was alive but also after his death. Of the two hundred bank accounts, only forty-five were ever located. It has been estimated that a sum in the neighborhood of $600,000 (1946 dollars) became Fields's inadvertent gift to the banks.

Anecdotes abound about the fabled super rich. Interestingly enough, many of them were niggardly with their money. S. S. Kresge, the dime-store magnate, reportedly kept his shoes long after they were worn out. He would line them with paper to extend their life. He was divorced twice, and both wives found him to be very stingy. H. L. Hunt, the oil billionaire, ate his lunches out of a desk drawer and fed inexpensive sandwiches to his luncheon guests. J. P. Getty, the billionaire entrepreneur, was said to have installed pay telephones in his mansion for the use of his guests.

These stories serve to underscore the fact that great wealth does not necessarily liberate anyone emotionally.

Symptoms of the Miser Headache

Listen to the miser and check any of the statements that apply to you:

☐ "All my life I have hoarded money. My family and friends have often commented on how much money I have stashed away."

The Miser's Misery 21

- ☐ "I am fascinated with money. I often hold on to funds rather than spend them, even though there is no particular reason to do so."
- ☐ "I don't usually admit to being niggardly. As a matter of fact, I am likely to justify my miserliness as being necessary, foresightful, and virtuous."
- ☐ "I have a terrible fear of losing funds and of being taken advantage of financially. Although I am often envious of other people's wealth, I tend to keep these feelings inside."
- ☐ "I have trouble enjoying the benefits of money and tend not to have much fun with cash. I'll spend money on necessities, but I resent using it for other purposes."
- ☐ "My friends and family are often angry with me about how little money I spend."
- ☐ "I don't know why I behave in a miserly way, although I usually tell myself it's for the money; I store money as a way to reduce my discomfort and anxiety, but I don't know what causes these feelings."
- ☐ "When someone asks why I behave as I do about money I reply, 'I feel as though something terrible is going to happen to me if I keep spending my money,' or 'I feel secure only when I hold onto my money.'"
- ☐ "I have difficulty trusting others and am often competitive. This trait makes it difficult for me to get along with people in general, not only in money matters."
- ☐ "I sometimes fail to take care of my health as well as I might because of my penny-pinching."

Assign one point to each item you checked. Find your total on the left-hand column of the Moneysanity Evaluation Chart. The middle column indicates your Fiscal Management Assessment (which describes your money problem situation), and the right-hand column lists recommended Green Therapies.

Moneysanity Evaluation: Miser

Severity of Headache	Fiscal Management Assessment	Helpful Green Therapies
7–10 points Splitting migraine	Holding on to funds is a way of life for you, and your "reasons" (rationalizations) are very set. Money isn't a pleasure, it's an obsession. You need help, but you may find it hard to make changes in your life.	Cognitive Behavior Therapy Destressing and Systematic Relaxation Psychodynamics Psychological Flashcards Thought Stopping
4–6 points Medium-range tension headache	Your money problems are less severe than they might be, but are still serious enough to prevent you from using your money effectively. Things are not good, but you might be open to modifying your ways.	Cognitive Behavior Therapy Destressing and Systematic Relaxation Letting Go Psychological Flashcards
1–3 points Mild cranial pain	You know what it means to be tight with your money but you also have some good times. When you are feeling more insecure you tend to get stingy, but you don't know why this happens. There's a good chance you can bring about changes.	Cognitive Behavior Therapy Destressing and Systematic Relaxation Letting Go Psychological Flashcards

Chapter 3
The Spendthrift Syndrome

Moneyanalysis Quiz Two: Are You an Overspender?

For each question, check the statement that most accurately describes your behavior. Upon completion, add up your score and refer to the explanation at the end of the test.

1. *If I have money to spend,*
   a. I occasionally splurge and overdo it, but more often than not it's no problem.
   b. I worry about whether to spend it. It's a struggle. Sometimes the overspending side wins and sometimes the control side wins.
   c. I think about how to spend it all the time. It gives me a real high. I love spending money, even though I overdo it.
   d. I'm never tempted to be extravagant. I always stick to my budget.
2. *I think credit cards are*
   a. useful to have, although I splurge with them once in a while.
   b. to be used only when I have to. I always pay the full amount on my bills, thus avoiding interest charges.
   c. the greatest invention in the world. I use them all the time, frequently to the limit and beyond.
   d. fun to have. I use them often and at times I tend to buy too much.
3. *When I go shopping,*
   a. I almost always buy just what I planned to get. Occasionally, I splurge on something I can't resist, but not often.
   b. I almost always buy more than I intended, but I don't feel good about it afterward.
   c. I often overspend and I usually feel good later.
   d. I stick to my shopping list and that makes me feel good.
4. *If I inherited a million dollars from a long-lost uncle,*
   a. I'd put most of it away in good investments after

consulting financial experts, but I'd keep some to spend for fun.
b. I'd put it all in the bank.
c. I'd go on a spending spree.
d. I'd buy all the things I've wanted for the past ten years, and I'd give money to my family and friends. Then I'd put the rest in the bank before deciding what else to buy.

5. *If I have a bad day at work,*
    a. I rarely buy myself a treat to make myself feel better.
    b. I always spend money to make myself feel better.
    c. I sometimes find I feel better if I spend money on myself.
    d. I would occasionally buy something to help me feel more secure.

6. *Do you sometimes go on a big shopping spree and spend a great deal of money in order to feel more alive and get a strong sense of relief afterward (perhaps almost a little sexual relief)?*
    a. Yes, often. I like buying things and I know what you mean by this kind of experience.
    b. Rarely. I hardly ever go on shopping sprees.
    c. That's ridiculous. I sometimes enjoy spending money freely but it's not a sexual experience. I never go on shopping sprees.
    d. Yes, absolutely. That's the way it is. There's a big buildup and then a moment of satisfaction.

7. *At the end of the month,*
    a. I often end up owing money and in debt, although I sometimes manage to stay one step ahead—at least for a while.
    b. I am always in debt.
    c. I usually can pay all my bills, although I occasionally go into debt.
    d. I never have outstanding bills. I spend only what I can afford and do not get into debt (excluding things like a mortgage and a car).

8. *Which statement do you identify most strongly with?*
    a. Some people consider me a spendthrift and I occasionally believe it's true.
    b. I am in good control of my finances and I have healthy attitudes toward buying and spending.
    c. I am learning to spend money within reasonable limits but I'm not there 100 percent yet.
    d. At least one of my parents had cash-control

problems handling money, and I've developed a real hangup about overspending.

9. *I use my credit card to buy things I wouldn't get if I were paying cash:*
   a. very rarely. I pay cash for everything except emergencies or in very special situations.
   b. too often, but I try to resist it.
   c. sometimes, but I prefer paying cash.
   d. all the time.

10. *When I feel anxious, bored, or angry,*
    a. I frequently spend money to alleviate my distress.
    b. I occasionally spend money to help me feel better.
    c. I always spend money to diminish these emotions.
    d. I never deal with these feelings by spending money.

Scoring Moneyanalysis Quiz Two: Spendthrift

Scoring Key

1. a. 2 points
   b. 1 point
   c. 0 points
   d. 3 points
2. a. 2 points
   b. 3 points
   c. 0 points
   d. 1 point
3. a. 2 points
   b. 0 points
   c. 1 point
   d. 3 points
4. a. 3 points
   b. 2 points
   c. 1 point
   d. 0 points
5. a. 3 points
   b. 0 points
   c. 1 point
   d. 2 points
6. a. 1 point
   b. 2 points
   c. 3 points
   d. 0 points
7. a. 1 point
   b. 0 points
   c. 2 points
   d. 3 points
8. a. 1 point
   b. 3 points
   c. 2 points
   d. 0 points
9. a. 3 points
   b. 1 point
   c. 2 points
   d. 0 points
10. a. 1 point
    b. 2 points
    c. 0 points
    d. 3 points

23–30 points
As you may have expected, you are not a compulsive overspender. You lean toward a balanced and sane approach.

15–22 points
This is a critical spread of points. If your score is at the higher end you are reasonably safe from this money headache. If it is at the lower end, you may have some problems. Read the chapter and follow the suggestions you find useful.

8–14 points
Your replies cluster heavily around the profile of an overspender. To correct this headache, your desire and motivation to change must be strong, and professional help may be warranted.

0–7 points
These scores suggest a confirmed spendthrift. Overspending is very much a part of your life. Altering this style requires conviction and patience. Follow all the chapter's suggestions and get professional help.

Compulsive spenders create one hell of a monetary headache for themselves and those around them. Uncontrolled spendthrifts have received growing attention in recent years and groups such as Shopaholics and Spendermenders have sprung up to help them.

A Case History: Joyce Spendthrift

When she got pregnant, Joyce didn't know that in less than a year her world would be unrecognizable. She had married at age nineteen to get away from an uncaring family. Superficially, her parents would help her, but they had a hard time giving. She had never received a regular allowance. Instead, she had saved the pennies friends and relatives gave her. She had learned that to feel good, she had to indulge herself, since little or no indulgence came from other people. For Joyce to experience generosity, she needed to create it herself. She used money to fill an inner void and allay her feelings of dissatisfaction.

For a couple of years after she married Mark, she remained in her pre-binge phase, trying with difficulty to maintain her overspending urges. It was only after Emily was born that Joyce developed a splitting monetary headache. Mark made a comfortable income as a computer salesman and he and Joyce had saved some money. Despite their security cushion, Mark was shocked to discover that Joyce had spent a small fortune on baby clothes and furniture for Emily. She overdosed on booties, sleepers, and diapers.

When Mark showed his annoyance, Joyce broke down. She never had nice things when she was little, she sobbed. Now she wanted them for her daughter.

This event seemed to unleash a barrage of compulsive spending behavior in Joyce, which left Mark furious, resentful, and hurt. It continued for several months, and eventually the couple separated.

Joyce was not as lucky as Gerald Tightwad. Her psychological hurts went deeper than his. Her primary fears were of rejection and loss of love. As she grew up, she felt unloved and, equally devastating, unlovable. Joyce tried to contain her anxieties by compulsively spending on herself and others. She inevitably reaped a harvest of guilt.

Emotionally, Joyce was very much a child—giving to herself because others failed to do so. The things she bought for her baby daughter were primarily for herself.

Joyce came to me for help and together we explored her neurotic situation. It soon became clear that she felt a great deal of anger toward her parents. Although she had at times been fed up with her parents' behavior, she hadn't been aware of her underlying hostility.

The hardest part of our work together was helping her to see the bad feelings she was carrying around about her parents. Once Joyce became more in touch with her "darker" feelings, I guided her toward lifting the blame she directed at her mother and father.

For Joyce to be free of her inner oppression—her sense of rejection and lack of love—she had to be willing to forgive her parents (see Chapter 12, Letting Go). With forgiveness would come psychological liberation. As long as she nurtured negative feelings, even on an unconscious level, Joyce would not be free to get on with her life.

Joyce had come to terms with the idea that overspending was a neurotic way of getting even with her parents for not having given her the love she needed. She had been using material things to buy other people's love, or to make herself feel worthy as a person.

We worked on relaxation exercises and also used Affirmations—positive statements—to build up her sense of worth. I would ask her, for example, to recite to herself daily statements such as: "I am a worthwhile person who has lovable qualities," or, "I don't have to overspend in order to be accepted." I also asked Joyce to practice imagining situations in which she spent a small sum of money. If she could learn to control her spending in her imagination, soon she would be able to do so in real-life situations.

Joyce made some gains but she continued to need to be vigilant and to exercise every bit of restraint she had.

Understanding the Spendthrift

Not all cases of out-of-control overspending are as extreme as Joyce's, but many have common elements. People with this money hangup are unhappy and dissatisfied. They apply an unconscious mechanism that Dr. Edmund Bergler, a famous psychoanalyst, calls "magic gestures." According to Bergler, "A magic gesture denotes an unconscious dramatization of the thought: 'I shall show you, bad mother and father, how I really wanted to be treated with kindness and generosity.' " Unfortunately, by trying to meet their emotional needs through neurotic mechanisms, overspenders may themselves feel guilty and alienate those close to them.

Compulsive spenders are comfortable only when they can spend almost as quickly as the need arises—which is often. This neurotic need is oriented toward spending for its own sake, and the underlying psychological reasons for it remain unknown to the "victim." Even though some of these people have financial resources and good jobs, they can never obtain all the spending money they feel driven to have.

Spendthrifts usually have a poor self-image and low self-esteem. They seem driven to put themselves into compromising situations that lead to debt, embarrassment, guilt, and anxiety. Their behavior often makes them dependent on others (those to whom they owe money and those who may want to bail them out). By doing so, they are symbolically saying "Take care of me," or even, "Save me." However, there is also a hostile and self-punishing side to the overspender's behavior. The hostility is expressed as an anger toward others, and the "punishment" occurs when the overspender seriously disrupts his life with his destructive behavior.

The spendthrift is usually overindulged and overprotected in childhood. Her parents may have substituted money for various forms of affection. As an adult, she overspends as a symbolic representation of that relationship. A variation on this theme can occur when the compulsive overspender seeks to compensate for a childhood in which both money and affection were in short supply. In this instance the person tries to create feelings that have been missing by purchasing "indulgences" via shopping sprees.

The buying is almost always an attempt to compensate for some lack or deprivation. The spendthrifts have a weak sense of self and excessive buying is, for them, a way to strengthen their identity. It's almost as if they changed the famous philosophical statement, "I think, therefore I am," to "I spend, therefore I am." Problem spenders express their unconscious emotional conflicts or feelings in their actions rather than in words. People have been known to be so needy that they have actually sent themselves flowers and gifts secretly while they were patients in a hospital. This sort of thing, of course, fails to get to the root of the problem.

Many people who know they have severe and addictive overspending problems won't do anything to stop themselves. They are like addicts who need their "fix." The "rush" they get from shopping is so important to them that they are not willing to give it up. Many will seek help only after they "bottom out" or have the wits scared out of them. Group therapy or a combination of group and individual therapy can be most effective in helping them.

Shopping Made Easy

Many businesses take advantage of compulsive overspenders by offering them television home-buying services and computer buying (which allows people to shop by selecting an item on the computer and putting their credit card number directly into the system). As a result of these modern innovations, there has been a steady increase in out-of-control neurotic shopping behavior.

Shopping malls and department-store complexes are, however, still the main haunts of the spendthrift. Many people are drawn to them as if by a magnet. The merchandise in individual stores plays an unimportant role in the appeal. It is not the products that count: it is being there and buying.

Help for the Spendthrift

On a recent NBC-TV *Today* program, participants in a self-help group called Spendermenders were interviewed. They spoke plaintively about their crippling addiction. They said their lives were in utter chaos while they were in their destructive spending phase. Just as an alcoholic cannot stop drinking, these people could not stop spending.

Spendermenders is a San Francisco-based, national mutual-support group dedicated to helping compulsive overspenders learn why they do what they do, what money is all about, how to handle it properly, and how not to sabotage themselves by destructive spending.

The association has learned one surprising thing from its fifteen hundred members: 80 percent of them are firstborn children! This statistic may suggest that firstborns are more vulnerable to the overspending malady or that they are the first to seek help. There are, of course, different possibilities.

The Ultimate Purchase

Uncontrolled buying is an activity that has lost its way, its reason for being. Of the many speculations about its inner meaning, one of the most insightful I have come across was written by the playwright Tennessee Williams in *Cat on a Hot Tin Roof*:

> Yes, sir, boy—the human animal is a beast that dies and if he's got money he buys and buys and buys and I think the reason he buys everything he can buy is that in the back of his mind he has the crazy hope that one of his purchases will be life everlasting!—which it never can be.

Perhaps to a degree we all unconsciously equate money with immortality. Perhaps spending money is a denial of death. Certainly, some psychoanalysts say that dreams of finding money are death-denying.

Symptoms of the Spendthrift Headache

Listen to the spendthrift and check any of the statements that apply to you.

- ☐ "My spending is frequently compulsive and out of control. I need to spend the way an addict needs a fix. I feel the need to spend continuously and often go on sprees or binges. I usually have little interest in the things after they are purchased, however."
- ☐ "I frequently run up large debts and I use my credit cards liberally. If I have any money left over at the end of the month, I usually spend it."
- ☐ "I often need to spend money when I feel depressed, under stress, worthless, afraid of being hurt, being along, or being rejected."
- ☐ "I often spend money as a way of providing instant gratification when what I actually want is love, recognition, or admiration."
- ☐ "When I buy things I feel positive about myself, but it never lasts. After it's all over, I go back to feeling guilty and unworthy."
- ☐ "I can't stop myself from spending, even though I feel guilt or shame afterward."
- ☐ "My family and friends are often annoyed and hurt by my overspending."
- ☐ "My spending problem is not serious, but I do tend to rely on credit cards and to pay only the minimum balance due. I also buy things on credit that I wouldn't buy when paying cash and I often don't have enough money around for emergencies."
- ☐ "Although I don't understand the real underlying anxieties, fears, and concerns that fuel my overspending, I often think that I could get out of debt if only I had more money."
- ☐ "Spending money makes me feel good in a way nothing else does."

Assign one point to each item you checked. Find your total on the left-hand column of the Moneysanity Evaluation Chart. The middle column indicates your Fiscal Management Assessment (which describes your money-problem situation), and the right-hand column lists recommended Green Therapies.

Moneysanity Evaluation: Spendthrift

Severity of Headache	Fiscal Management Assessment	Helpful Green Therapies
7–10 points Splitting migraine	Your overspending is having a detrimental effect on your life. A great deal of conviction, determination, and motivation will be needed before you can change. You may need professional help, and group therapy may be helpful.	Cognitive Behavior Therapy Destressing and Systematic Relaxation Psychodynamics Psychological Flashcards Thought Stopping
4–6 points Medium-range tension headache	Your uncontrolled spending is interfering significantly with your efforts to use money realistically. Make a commitment to help yourself or to get help from others. Group therapy may be very helpful.	Cognitive Behavior Therapy Destressing and Systematic Relaxation Letting Go Psychodynamics Psychological Flashcards
1–3 points Mild cranial pain	You have spendthrift tendencies but you have control over them. The problem may tend to flare up at stressful times in your life. You should be able to improve your spending habits.	Cognitive Behavior Therapy Destressing and Systematic Relaxation Letting Go Psychological Flashcards

Chapter 4
The Tycoon's Trauma

Moneyanalysis Quiz Three:
Is Money Extremely Important To You?

For each question, check the statement that most accurately describes your behavior. Upon completion, add up your score and refer to the explanation at the end of the test.

1. *If I had my way, I'd talk about money-making ideas and schemes*
   a. just about 100 percent of the time.
   b. very frequently.
   c. on occasion.
   d. rarely.
2. *If I inherited some money,*
   a. I would invest most of it and spend just a little bit.
   b. I would invest some and buy things with the rest.
   c. I would spend some, invest some, put some in savings, and share the remainder with those close to me.
   d. I would invest it all. Later I would reinvest the earnings from the capital.
3. *If I had enough money to meet my needs and a little bit more,*
   a. I might occasionally think about ways to make more money.
   b. I would be content.
   c. I would still try to increase my bank account.
   d. I would remain preoccupied with building my finances.
4. *If someone asked me if I agreed that money can make me happy—the more the better, I would reply:*
   a. "Yes, I believe it."
   b. "No, I don't believe it."
   c. "It's sometimes true for me."
   d. "It's rarely true for me."
5. *The size of my bank balance*
   a. is very important to me, and it runs my life at times.
   b. is vitally important to me. Increasing my money motivates everything I do.
   c. is only one factor of many in my overall financial thinking.
   d. sometimes absorbs my thoughts.

6. *I think about money*
   a. fairly often.
   b. only when a money matter comes up.
   c. occasionally.
   d. a number of times a day. In fact, I'm sort of obsessed by it.
7. *When I'm with wealthy people,*
   a. I soon forget how rich they are.
   b. I become absorbed with their success and it makes me want to redouble my efforts to amass money.
   c. I think about their wealth on and off and it makes me uncomfortable.
   d. I act as I would with anyone else.
8. *I believe that how much money a person has*
   a. is important up to a point but is not the only way to judge a person.
   b. is a poor way to judge the person.
   c. is very important. Money is the ultimate symbol of success.
   d. shows how successful the person is in some areas.
9. *Acquiring a lot of money would make me feel*
   a. powerful.
   b. richer, but not much different.
   c. lucky.
   d. better than I do now.
10. *If I knew that my money was growing substantially every day, it would make me feel secure because*
    a. money is useful.
    b. it helps to have a lot of money.
    c. accumulating a great deal of money is the most important thing to me.
    d. we all need money to help run our lives.

Scoring Moneyanalysis Quiz Three: Tycoon

Scoring Key

1. a. 0 points
   b. 1 point
   c. 2 points
   d. 3 points
2. a. 1 point
   b. 2 points
   c. 3 points
   d. 0 points
3. a. 2 points
   b. 3 points
   c. 1 point
   d. 0 points
4. a. 0 points
   b. 3 points
   c. 1 point
   d. 2 points
5. a. 1 point
   b. 0 points
   c. 3 points
   d. 2 points
6. a. 1 point
   b. 3 points
   c. 2 points
   d. 0 points
7. a. 2 points
   b. 0 points
   c. 1 point
   d. 3 points
8. a. 2 points
   b. 3 points
   c. 0 points
   d. 1 point
9. a. 0 points
   b. 2 points
   c. 3 points
   d. 1 point
10. a. 2 points
    b. 1 point
    c. 0 points
    d. 3 points

23–30 points
You are interested in money but you are not obsessed with piling it in endless heaps. Read the chapter anyway, for your own interest.

15–22 points
The closer your score is to fifteen the more severe your headache— and the more you should consider reassessing the role of money in your life.

8–14 points
Your constant thoughts about money are not healthy. Money has probably become an end in itself. You may find this chapter helpful.

0–7 points
You have the characteristics of a fanatical money-maker. Making money is probably interfering with your personal life and relationships. Do what you can to establish a better balance in your life, and, if necessary, get help in order to do so.

The craving for limitless gold has been with us since time immemorial, although America, more than any other country in the world, has turned the quest into a way of life. Alexis de Tocqueville, the nineteenth-century commentator on the United States and author of *Democracy in America*, observed: "The love of money is either the chief or secondary motive at the bottom of everything Americans do."

Given the obsessive drive some people have toward the accumulation of money, one might almost think it was an inborn need. Thomas Wiseman, author of *The Money Motive*, sums it up:

> There is nothing in biological necessity to account for the drive to get rich, nor is there any equivalent for it in animal life. It is something that serves no fundamental purpose, and it does not fulfill any basic need; indeed, by definition to "get rich" is to get more than one needs. And yet this seemingly purposeless drive is one of the most powerful known to man, and it is probable that people have done more injuries to each other in the name of money, than for any other reason.

A Case History: Richard Tycoon

Anyone observing Richard's life would quickly recognize the symptoms of the tycoon mentality. I knew he was in trouble as soon as I heard him tell his wife, Gail, that the reason he was working twenty-three hours a day, six days a week, in the family wholesale-hardware business was so they would eventually have the millions that would enable him to retire at age forty-five. Gail tried to make it clear that by then she and the two children would be long gone.

Gail and Richard had been childhood sweethearts and had married right after they finished college. She had always been interested in nursing, and he in law. However, his father was able to convince him to turn away from law school and join the family's hardware business instead. Soon he became obsessed with increasing the company's profits. At first, Richard made what he believed were concessions to his family: he spent a night or two each week with his wife and Saturday afternoons with the kids. But that ended, and eventually all he could see before his eyes were dollar bills.

When the situation became extreme, Gail threatened divorce. Richard was hurt and angry. He couldn't understand why Gail didn't appreciate the sacrifices he was making for her and the children. His monetary headache was giving him double vision and he could no longer see clearly.

In therapy, Richard revealed that he had always been very competitive with his father. As a child, Richard had constantly heard how successful his father was in business. Everything was sacrificed on behalf of the business. Indeed, Richard seldom saw his father during his school years. Money was talked about a great deal in Richard's family, but the emphasis was always on having it rather than spending it. Richard fantasized about how he would build his fortune—and it would be far bigger than his father's.

At one time he had planned to prove his superiority to his father by becoming a big-time, hotshot lawyer. Joining the family business was an even better way to accomplish his long-term fantasy, and when the opportunity arose, he jumped at the chance.

Another factor that aggravated the situation was the general decline in communication between Richard and Gail. Richard resented Gail's lack of support for his fortune-building plans, and he stayed away from her more than he had to, in order to hurt her. He justified his actions by falling back on his story that he was working for her. In one sense, he was doing it for her, but he was also punishing her for what he considered to be her lack of loyalty.

Helping Richard with his monetary headache was tricky because he came to see me to help him win Gail back. He thought he could learn to act in ways that would convince her that this outlook was right. He didn't really come for himself at all.

Helping the Money-maker

In order to turn a problem situation around, there must always be three basic elements present: an acknowledgement that a difficulty exists, an agreement as to what it is, and the willingness and motivation to change it. Richard agreed there was a problem, but he believed that it was Gail's.

The first thing we did was to role-play the situation. This very useful exercise helps a person to know what it feels like to be in another person's shoes. At first, I played Gail's role and tried to get Richard to see things from my (Gail's) point of view. Then we reversed roles and Richard played Gail's role.

Richard was resistant and skeptical initially, but soon he began to realize that the situation was not one-sided. It wasn't just a question of showing Gail how wrong she was. Maybe he had to change his position, also.

Next we explored Richard's relationship with his father. He discovered that his anger and sense of competition with his father ruled much of his money-building behavior. We also took a look at his value system. He was shocked to realize that his life was totally dedicated to money. He had thought that family life and parenting were the uppermost values in his life. Gradually, Richard understood that he had to make some conscious choices in his life. He couldn't have everything; he would have to give up something.

He eventually chose his family, but his need to strive and overachieve financially didn't completely leave him. He and Gail continued to work hard to keep their marriage going.

Understanding the Money-maker

Fanatical money-makers have a fascinating trait in common. They love to see their dollars do arithmetic acrobatics: jump up and up, multiply, and perform feats of endless proliferation. Most of all, they enjoy watching the money they own reproduce itself, thus confirming what has become a maxim in our time: money breeds money.

People expect fabulous things from dollars. They are almost always disappointed. Adam Smith, in *The Money Game*, provides charming relish on this food for thought: he titles his seventh chapter "An Anthem From George Frederick Handel: When I Am

Rich Then Shall All Things Change, And My Life Be Different." This certainly suggests high expectations from monetary sources which the statistics concerning lottery winners, for example, do not bear out.

Fanatical money-makers are usually unconscious of their money neurosis. The fact that it is socially acceptable to pursue money makes it even harder for them to realize they have a problem. The tragedy for the money-maker occurs when it becomes clear that she is the prisoner of the money-making genie, and not the other way around. She cannot stop herself from making more money (like a sorcerer's apprentice filling endless buckets with dollar bills), but simultaneously money ceases to have any real meaning to her. Money has become more important than what it can buy and more important than those nearest and dearest to the money-maker.

Symptoms of the Tycoon Headache

Listen to the tycoon and check any of the statements that apply to you.

- ☐ "I am not very interested in spending money, but I love to amass it."
- ☐ "Even when I have more money than I need, I still work at increasing my stockpiles."
- ☐ "For as long as I can remember, I have been interested in making money."
- ☐ "I am always looking over my shoulder to find out if I am doing better than others."
- ☐ "I rarely think about what money will buy for me. As a matter of fact, sometimes I wonder what it is all about."
- ☐ "My family resents my absorption with money-making."
- ☐ "When I am not involved in money, I often feel anxious for no reason."
- ☐ "Sometimes I worry that I am too absorbed with making money, but I soon forget about it when I realize how well I blend in with others who do the same thing."

☐ "I often think that the more money I have, the better control I'll have over my world and the happier I'll be. At other times, I think I'm doing all this for my family, so when there's enough money I'll be able to be with them. I'll stop working then."
☐ "Money is the best way to gain power, status, and approval."

Assign one point to each item you checked. Find your total on the left-hand column of the Moneysanity Evaluation Chart. The middle column indicates your Fiscal Management Assessment (which describes your money-problem situation), and the right-hand column lists recommended Green Therapies.

Moneysanity Evaluation: The Tycoon

Severity of Headache	Fiscal Management Assessment	Helpful Green Therapies
7–10 points Splitting migraine	Thoughts about money and amassing it pervade your mind. Money has become a kind of religion and its real purpose and function are forgotten. Some change is possible, but motivation must be very high.	Cognitive Behavior Therapy Destressing and Systematic Relaxation Psychodynamics Psychological Flashcards Thought Stopping
4–6 points Medium-range tension headache	You are preoccupied with piling up funds but able at times to see the harmful effects. If the will to change is present, you can modify your behavior	Cognitive Behavior Therapy Destressing and Systematic Relaxation Psychodynamics Psychological Flashcards Thought Stopping
1–3 points Mild cranial pain	Your problems are not as chronic as in the other categories and are more amenable to change.	Cognitive Behavior Therapy Destressing and Systematic Relaxation Psychodynamics (Brief) Psychological Flashcards

Chapter 5
The Bargainer's Bug

Moneyanalysis Quiz Four:
Are You a Compulsive Hunter of Bargains?

For each question, check the statement that most accurately describes your behavior. Upon completion, add up your score and refer to the explanation at the end of the test.

1. *If I see a store that is having a big sale where there are lots of good deals,*
   a. I will buy something if I need it. Otherwise I'll pass it by.
   b. I would certainly go into the store and would probably buy whatever was a good deal.
   c. I go in if I have the time. I enjoy a sale if it's easily accessible.
   d. I might see what there was, but I don't mind missing a sale. It's not something that matters to me.
2. *I like a bargain because*
   a. it occasionally makes me feel cleverer.
   b. I like to feel I made a good deal.
   c. it is fun to outsmart the seller.
   d. I like to save money.
3. *When I buy something, I look for*
   a. the best bargain I can get, even if the workmanship is not great.
   b. more than my money's worth.
   c. a bargain, but it's not that important.
   d. value for my money, but cost is only one of many factors.
4. *When I get an item for a low price,*
   a. I am pleased, especially if the item was something I really wanted.
   b. I'm usually excited, no matter what I bought.
   c. I get a real thrill.
   d. it matters very little to me. What I care about is the actual acquisition.
5. *If I had a choice between buying a valuable object at a reasonable price and a less valuable object at a giveaway price,*
   a. I would definitely take the reasonable price.
   b. I would lean toward the reasonable price.

c. I would lean toward the giveaway price.
   d. I would definitely take the giveaway price.
6. *I pay the full price for things*
   a. only if I absolutely have to.
   b. quite often. Price is not the main factor.
   c. usually, but I'd rather not.
   d. occasionally.
7. *I don't know why it happens, but I get a strong sense of elation when I get a great bargain.*
   a. This is exactly how I feel. In fact, I've felt that way as long as I can remember.
   b. This is infrequently the case for me.
   c. This is not me. What matters is the quality, the workmanship, and the design.
   d. This is quite close to the mark, but it varies in different situations.
8. *When I buy gifts for friends,*
   a. I try to find something my friends will like, but mostly I look for a bargain.
   b. cost is unimportant. I enjoy buying presents that my friends will like.
   c. I think about the price only occasionally.
   d. my main criterion is cost.
9. *Do people think you are too preoccupied with getting a good deal for your money?*
   a. Not at all.
   b. Occasionally.
   c. Rarely.
   d. Definitely. Some think it, and the rest actually tell me.
10. *If I bought something on sale, but ended up not using it,*
   a. I'd be annoyed with myself.
   b. I would be surprised. I never buy things I don't need.
   c. I wouldn't be surprised. I get more pleasure from getting a good deal than from my purchases.
   d. I wouldn't care. I always get a real sense of triumph from buying things at a fabulous price whether I use them afterward or not.

Scoring Moneyanalysis Quiz Four: Bargainer

Scoring Key

1. a. 3 points
   b. 0 points
   c. 1 point
   d. 2 points
2. a. 1 point
   b. 2 points
   c. 0 points
   d. 3 points
3. a. 0 points
   b. 1 point
   c. 2 points
   d. 3 points
4. a. 1 point
   b. 2 points
   c. 0 points
   d. 3 points
5. a. 3 points
   b. 2 points
   c. 1 point
   d. 0 points
6. a. 0 points
   b. 3 points
   c. 2 points
   d. 1 point
7. a. 0 points
   b. 2 points
   c. 3 points
   d. 1 point
8. a. 1 point
   b. 3 points
   c. 2 points
   d. 0 points
9. a. 3 points
   b. 1 point
   c. 2 points
   d. 0 points
10. a. 2 points
    b. 3 points
    c. 1 point
    d. 0 points

23–30 points
You may enjoy the odd bargain but you are not carried away by the process. Bargains can be fun, and that's that.

15–22 points
The closer your score is to 15, the farther you are leaning toward compulsive bargain hunting. Be sure you don't catch the bug. Read the chapter and help yourself.

8–14 points
You are getting into dangerous territory. Your bargain hunting is getting out of control. Follow the suggestions and see what you can do on your own behalf to change. Get help if you need it.

0–7 points
Your score indicates strong compulsive bargain-hunting behavior. It's not so easy to alter your ways, but it can be done. Work at it, and also seek professional assistance.

Who do you know who can climb tall buildings in a single leap, crush others who get in their way, and pay any price to get the job done? Yes, you're right, it's the invincible bargainer. And his or her monetary headache is worthy of Superman, since this cranial pain is actually a combination of two other soreheads—the tightwad and the spendthrift. The bargain hunter is capable of squeezing money so hard that it screams for another owner.

Symptoms of the Bargainer's Bug

The signs of this malady are quite clear. Paying the full price for anything is taken as a personal affront and defeat. The dyed-in-the-wool haggler swoops down on the less expensive item like a pelican spearing its dinner in rough waters. It may be the most ridiculous and unnecessary purchase in the world. What counts is that the buyer gets a great deal, that the price is less than usual, that money is being saved, that the seller is outsmarted, that others would pay more for the item in a regular sale, and that the bargainer gets a big thrill in the whole snaring process. These are the telltale signals.

A Case History: Sarah Bargainer

Sarah grew up in Europe. Her mother died when she was very young, leaving her feeling insecure and anxious. When she was nineteen, she and her sisters and brother came to America with the dream of improving their lives. Sarah worked long hours for little money and met her husband-to-be shortly after her arrival.

Adam was a happy-go-lucky, easy-going, passive sort of guy. He taught music, and they started their life together with limited finances. Sarah, however, was a magician with money. Adam gave her one dollar and she appeared to turn it into two! She could stretch her money beyond anyone's wildest expectations. The problem was that often the trick was on her.

She was frequently moody and petulant. The pleasure she got from outsmarting sellers was short-lived. She often ended up buying goods that fell apart. Once she bought several handbags, only to store them away in a closet and never use any of them.

Sarah took pride in her ability to get bargains wherever she went. Often the product was inferior, but that did not seem to matter to her as much as putting one over on the seller, and buying the item for less than her neighbor paid.

In some cases, Adam suffered the consequences of his wife's distorted behavior. For example, when he wanted to buy an air conditioner one sweltering summer, Sarah insisted that he leave the matter in her hands. She came home with a super-special sell-out model—the bargain of the month. It was a brand that no one had ever heard of, and unfortunately it broke down within weeks of its purchase.

The psychological reasons behind Sarah's monetary headache relate to her early childhood. After the death of her mother, she was cared for by older and somewhat indifferent siblings and a stern father. Later, her father remarried, but her new stepmother was an unkind and uneducated woman who failed to provide Sarah with a sense of security, safety, or contentment.

As a result, Sarah began neurotically trying to gain the love and affection she missed by paying less money for things than others did. Getting a bargain made her feel special, as though she were finally getting her share of what she had lost as a child. It's as if the driven bargainer interprets the seller's lowering of his price as a caring act. The neurotic logic might be: "If he didn't favor me, why else would he give me a bargain?" Her motivation was, of course, unconscious.

Understanding the Bargain Hunter

Most bargainers become so embroiled in their battle of wits with the seller that they don't realize they are really throwing away their money. In their endless need to outsmart others, they lose sight of the fact that they really don't need the thing they're buying.

Typically, what the bargain hunter is left with is his memory (fantasy) of how he outwitted the seller. That memory seems to be much more important to him than the actual purchases, since it would seem that in some way it helps him to feel invulnerable. By acting aggressively in his purchases, the bargainer protects himself from possible rejection. In the past, he felt helpless to avoid the psychological pain of rejection. Now he outsmarts others as a way of lowering his anxiety level. The ultimate goal for the bargainer is to get something (love) for nothing (without having to buy it).

Helping the Bargainer

Getting a good deal was a form of positive recognition for Sarah, and she was very reluctant to give it up. What she needed was to become aware of the wasteful and destructive side of her behavior. She had developed her neurotic money habits over a period of years to bolster her low self-esteem. Although she wanted attention and affection from others, she grew afraid to ask for them. Sarah had to learn how to request the emotional nurturing she needed in a direct way.

In therapy, Sarah learned to understand her money behavior. We first explored her early emotional relationships. Then we used fantasy and imagination to examine her internal feelings. I asked her to collect pictures of people shopping and to fantasize about buying things that were not bargains. Since the non-bargainer role made her anxious, I taught her progressive relaxation techniques. She soon became quite proficient at bringing about a peaceful, inner calm. By saying the word "calm" out loud at home and silently in public, she was able to recall feelings of serenity.

Her husband, Adam, became actively involved in her therapy. Sarah was encouraged to ask him freely and frequently for praise and affection. She resumed an earlier hobby, painting, and Adam was effusive in his sincerely felt compliments.

Gradually, Sarah went on fewer bargaining binges, and she practiced buying items that she needed without extended haggling.

The Bargainer's Bug

She still tried to buy things at what she thought were good prices, but the pressures and the negative behavior were greatly reduced.

Symptoms of the Bargainer's Headache

Listen to the bargainer and check any of the statements that apply to you.

- ☐ "When I shop, I must feel that I'm saving money and that the price was less than usual."
- ☐ "I enjoy knowing that others pay more for things."
- ☐ "I can't resist a sale of almost any kind and I often end up buying things just because they are bargains. Many of these purchases get little or no use."
- ☐ "The thought of paying the full price for anything revolts me."
- ☐ "As a child, I felt emotionally shortchanged. When I find a bargain, I feel that someone cares for me."
- ☐ "Getting things for less money makes me feel superior. I sometimes feel a desperate need to be treated in this special way."
- ☐ "Getting a great deal helps me alleviate feelings of insecurity and vulnerability."
- ☐ "I spend a lot of time, energy, and thought on my money-saving pursuits."
- ☐ "I can't stand paying the asking price for anything. It makes me feel bad about myself if I do."
- ☐ "I feel that there's something wrong with me if I can't get the seller to come down significantly in price."

Assign one point to each item you checked. Find your total on the left-hand column of the Moneysanity Evaluation Chart. The middle column indicates your Fiscal Management Assessment (which describes your money-problem situation), and the right-hand column lists recommended Green Therapies.

Moneysanity Evaluation: The Bargainer

Severity of Headache	Fiscal Management Assessment	Helpful Green Therapies
7–10 points Splitting migraine	Hardly a day goes by without a bargain hunt. The drive to get a little extra or something for less dominates your life. Your money attitudes are out of control. A lot of help is needed.	Assertive Behavior Training Cognitive Behavior Therapy Destressing and Systematic Relaxation Psychodynamics Psychological Flashcards Thought Stopping
4–6 points Medium-range tension headache	You tend to be insecure and to look for that extra "something." It's a quest without a "grail." There's always one more bargain to seek out. It's quite hard to modify these attitudes without a sense of readiness and determination.	Assertive Behavior Training (Brief) Cognitive Behavior Therapy Destressing and Systematic Relaxation Psychodynamics (Brief) Psychological Flashcards Thought Stopping
1–3 points Mild cranial pain	Yours is a more flexible money handling position—but you are still a bargain hunter.	Cognitive Behavior Therapy (Brief) Destressing and Systematic Relaxation Psychological Flashcards Thought Stopping

Chapter 6
The Gambler's Grippe

Moneyanalysis Quiz Five:
Do You Suffer from the Gambler's Grippe?

For each question, check the statement that most accurately describes your behavior. Upon completion, add up your score and refer to the explanation at the end of the test.

1. *When I wager my money—be it on the stock market or in a gambling casino—I feel*
   a. a little bit excited, but I can stop gambling if I want to.
   b. caught up in it but I can stop.
   c. extremely involved and I can hardly stop.
   d. mildly interested but not excited. I enjoy social gambling once in a while.

2. *For me, the main purpose of money is to*
   a. use it in a rational manner.
   b. get enjoyment. To me that means playing cards for money or similar social gambling as often as I can.
   c. wager it in one form or another and to show how lucky I am in my efforts.
   d. take care of my basic needs using sound financial planning.

3. *If I lost a lot of money at cards,*
   a. it wouldn't usually make much difference. I'd probably still play again.
   b. it wouldn't stop me from playing again.
   c. I might get discouraged from gambling again.
   d. it would be a long time before I played again—if I ever did.

4. *When I go to the racetrack,*
   a. I only occasionally place a bet because I feel lucky.
   b. I always take my lucky charm.
   c. I frequently feel lucky.
   d. I use reason and logic to decide which horse to bet on.

5. *I gamble with money*
   a. only occasionally.
   b. very rarely.
   c. whenever I can.
   d. often.

6. *When I see a play, read a book, or watch a movie about a gambler,*
   a. I do not identify with the gambler at all.
   b. I strongly identify with the gambler.
   c. I frequently identify with the gambler.
   d. I sometimes identify with the gambler.
7. *If I suddenly found a sum of money that wasn't traceable to its owner, the chances are I would*
   a. divide it up into my different bank accounts.
   b. save some of it.
   c. place a bet of some kind.
   d. spend half and gamble the other half.
8. *I have gambled a lot of money in order to recoup a big loss*
   a. two or three times in my life.
   b. never. I gamble very infrequently, and only for small stakes.
   c. maybe once.
   d. a number of times.
9. *Do you tend to view events in terms of odds (for example, the odds of inflation going up in the next six months, the odds of the home team winning or of the price of gold dropping)?*
   a. Yes, on any number of occasions.
   b. Yes, I've been known to react this way.
   c. No, never.
   d. Yes, all the time.
10. *If I were to rate my interest in gambling—be it cards, horses, or stocks—I would say:*
    a. it's extremely high—at times I'm preoccupied with it. I take it quite seriously.
    b. I get into it when I get the chance—sometimes that can be often.
    c. it's more than average—but I don't think much about it in between.
    d. it's very average, very casual. I bet occasionally just for fun.

Scoring Moneyanalysis Quiz Five: Gambler

Scoring Key

1. a. 2 points
   b. 1 point
   c. 0 points
   d. 3 points
2. a. 3 points
   b. 1 point
   c. 0 points
   d. 2 points
3. a. 1 point
   b. 0 points
   c. 2 points
   d. 3 points
4. a. 2 points
   b. 0 points
   c. 1 point
   d. 3 points
5. a. 2 points
   b. 3 points
   c. 0 points
   d. 1 point
6. a. 3 points
   b. 0 points
   c. 1 point
   d. 2 points
7. a. 3 points
   b. 2 points
   c. 0 points
   d. 1 point
8. a. 1 point
   b. 3 points
   c. 2 points
   d. 0 points
9. a. 1 point
   b. 2 points
   c. 3 points
   d. 0 points
10. a. 0 points
    b. 1 point
    c. 2 points
    d. 3 points

23–30 points
You are not the gambling type, although you may indulge once in a while. Gambling is not your money problem.

15–22 points
The closer your score is to 15 the more serious your problem is. Yours is still not necessarily a serious situation, but the leanings seem to be there.

8–14 points
Because the gambling headache can be quite severe, you should get help soon. If you are highly motivated, try some of the advice in the book and then seek professional assistance.

0–7 points
Your score signifies a full gambler-type profile. Try the help suggested in the book with the assistance of family, group support, and professionals who specialize in the field.

There are probably neurotic elements in all forms of gambling but it's basically a question of degree. Most people can take it or leave it. They gamble for fun and enjoyment. The professional gambler, of course, bets as a means of earning a living and therefore as a way of life.

It is the compulsive gambler who has a serious psychological problem. He's an addict: he can't stop. The elements of chance, luck, unpredictability, and risk play major roles in luring him to disaster.

Unhealthy gambling is ruled by unconscious needs. Judging from the desperate way gamblers throw money away (often in order to recoup previous losses), it appears that they have a strong drive to lose their funds. Long-standing gamblers have a saying: if to gamble and win is the greatest thrill you can have, to gamble and lose is the second greatest.

Serious problem gamblers are damned both ways. If they continue to gamble, they inevitably suffer. If they stop gambling for a little while, their lives feel empty and meaningless.

A Case History: Larry Gamble

Larry couldn't get the gambling "monkey" off his back. He was one of six siblings and had married Lenore when she was nineteen and he was twenty-four years old. He and his young bride had the first of their four children a year later. Lenore was immature and quite emotionally dependent upon Larry. Larry subsequently felt pressured and tense.

When he was in his teens, Larry played poker with his friends for small stakes, but he never gambled much. One day after work his desire to increase his earnings led him to the track. Later that evening, he returned home waving two hundred dollars in his hand. He told Lenore he had won because he had been carrying his good-luck charm, a coin Lenore had given him when they met. She felt proud of her role in Larry's winnings. They celebrated that evening with a big night on the town.

Larry began to visit the track at least three times a week. At first, he didn't do too badly. Lenore grew angry about the amount of time he spent away from home but she relented every time he came home with extra cash.

Inevitably the bubble burst. Larry began to lose—a little at first, then more and more. Eventually he had to dip into their savings. He began to lie to Lenore about what was happening, telling her that Lady Luck would favor him soon. His most repeated line was, "Tomorrow I'll win."

Eventually, Larry's fantasies and daydreams were preoccupied with betting and winning back the money he had lost. His relationship with Lenore deteriorated, and he shared fewer of the responsibilities at home, adding to the domestic friction. Things got so bad that he and Lenore finally had to separate for a while.

Understanding the Gambler

The features that identify serious gamblers are a sense of feeling chosen, a belief that they can control fate, the use of superstition to support gambling, the exhilaration of risk taking, and the complete unawareness of how the obsession has taken over. The sad irony of this condition is that it is generally agreed that the gambler's unconscious aim is to lose.

Trying to recoup gambling losses becomes a downward spiral of self-destruction. A stock-market gambler who was asked how good he was at limiting the amount of money he used to gamble replied: "Hell, I've lost seven thousand dollars trying to win back fifty bucks."

Gamblers are always seeking to prove that life's odds are in their favor. It's as if they are using money to tell their fortunes.

Helping the Gambler

Larry eventually began to realize the damage he had done and he agreed to go to meetings with gamblers who were having similar problems. Shortly thereafter he came to me for private counseling, and his life began to improve. Larry was one of the lucky ones; many gamblers find changing practically impossible.

After I worked with Larry for several months, it became clear that he had some strong negative feelings toward Lenore. He felt tied down by her and he resented her overdependency on him.

Larry admitted that although he tried to win when he gambled, he also got a perverse pleasure from losing. He had felt guilty about these feelings because he knew how much it upset Lenore when he lost.

Finally, he realized that losing was a way of expressing his anger at Lenore. His losses hurt her as much or more than they hurt him. Larry's behavior may appear to be paradoxical at first glance, but in fact people often hurt themselves when they attempt to hurt someone else.

Lenore and Larry had certain strengths in their marriage but good communication skills were not among them. Larry had to learn to risk discovering things—like Lenore's overdependency—that she didn't want to discuss. Once their communication skills improved, Lenore and Larry's marriage improved as well as did Larry's gambling problem.

Some of the Green Therapies that particularly helped Larry were: Letting Go, Cognitive Behavior Therapy, and Creating Your Own Dictionary.

Famous Gamblers

Gambling is seen by many as glamorous and romantic. This association is helped by the many famous people who were gamblers.

A notorious example was a beautiful Polish film star who was also mistress of the famous movie mogul, Darryl F. Zanuck. Her name was Bella Darvi. It has been said that at the dramatic height of her gambling sickness—after she had lost all her money—she boldly threw her diamond rings on the betting table to cover her debts. Zanuck bailed her out innumerable times, but even he eventually gave up. She finally killed herself.

One of the most famous writers of all time was also a pathological gambler. In his novel, *The Gambler*, Fyodor Dostoyevski creates an eerie parallel to his own life:

> In five minutes I accumulated 400 gold pieces at roulette. I should have left at that moment, but a strange feeling came over me to challenge Fate. It was the wish to give Fate a punch in the nose and show her my tongue.

Dostoyevski was hopelessly caught up in a web of lies, deceits, false promises, renunciations, self-accusations, guilt, and retribution. Nothing seemed to help—he gambled until he lost everything. The temptations of gambling totally swallowed him up.

Symptoms of the Gambler's Headache

Listen to the gambler and check any of the statements that apply to you.
- ☐ "I love to take chances."
- ☐ "Placing a bet makes me feel exhilarated and optimistic."
- ☐ "I feel chosen when luck comes my way, and I am superstitious when I gamble."
- ☐ "When I am winning—be it at cards, at the racetrack, or on the stock market—I find it nearly impossible to stop."
- ☐ "I have trouble handling risk whenever I gamble."
- ☐ "Even if I lose, I don't stop gambling."
- ☐ "Gambling makes me feel powerful, something I don't feel at other times."
- ☐ "I often feel guilty and unsure of myself."
- ☐ "When I gamble I feel a sense of power, as if each win is a major victory."
- ☐ "I started gambling shortly after a crisis or a period of stress in my life."

Assign one point to each item you checked. Find your total on the left-hand column of the Moneysanity Evaluation Chart. The middle column indicates your Fiscal Management Assessment (which describes your money-problem situation), and the right-hand column lists recommended Green Therapies.

Moneysanity Evaluation: Gambler

Severity of Headache	Fiscal Management Assessment	Helpful Green Therapies
7–10 points Splitting migraine	Gambling plays a major role in your life. It's excessive and has addictive elements. Money is often an end in itself, and winning seems to be the only real goal. A gambling orientation permeates other areas of your life. Changing at this level is equivalent to conquering alcohol or drug addiction. It's very hard, but not impossible. It requires outside assistance and family support.	Assertive Behavior Training Cognitive Behavior Therapy Destressing and Systematic Relaxation Letting Go Psychodynamics Psychological Flashcards Thought Stopping
4–6 points Medium-range tension headache	You are controlled by gambling, but not quite to the degree of the extreme group. You may not be aware of the psychological problems. To change you will need to be motivated and to have help from others.	Assertive Behavior Training Cognitive Behavior Therapy Destressing and Systematic Relaxation Letting Go Psychodynamics Psychological Flashcards Thought Stopping

(continued on next page)

The Gambler's Grippe

Severity of Headache	Fiscal Management Assessment	Helpful Green Therapies
1–3 points Mild cranial pain	Your situation is the much more common or "garden variety." It can get out of control and present some problems but it ordinarily isn't serious. Your tendencies may get in the way of effective money management. You need support to keep your gambling in safe limits at times.	Cognitive Behavior Therapy Destressing and Systematic Relaxation Psychological Flashcards Thought Stopping

PART II
The Green Therapies:
Banishing Monetary Headaches

Many of us behave neurotically in the handling of our financial affairs. These actions prevent us from enjoying our cash and using it effectively. But before we can change our behavior, we need to understand how these interferences operate and what we can do to remove them.

By taking the Moneyanalysis quizzes, you have been able to learn which money headache you have. The Moneysanity evaluations described the severity of the pain and listed the remedial approaches you needed to follow to achieve Moneysanity.

The Green Therapies are psychological techniques that have been adapted to money behavior problems. They have been useful in my work with clients, and they will be helpful to you.

There are literally hundreds of psychotherapies—from Morita therapy, which is a Japanese method that goes through four stages from absolute bed rest deprived of all distractions on to full work, to horticultural therapy, which uses gardening to produce beneficial changes in the client's emotional state. All these therapies, no matter how diverse, share a common goal: to make clients feel more whole, peaceful, fulfilled, and at one with themselves. Unfortunately, however, too many therapists present their particular technique with the blind conviction of a zealot and an attempt to force everyone onto a therapeutic procrustean couch. My position is, if the therapy doesn't fit, don't wear it.

All forms of psychological healing have helped some people at one time or another. In fact, to borrow from Abraham Lincoln, I would say that some of the therapies help all of the people some of the time, and all of the therapies help some of the people all of the time, but none of the therapies helps all of the people all of the time. The success of a therapy depends on your own therapy goals and your motivation, faith, belief, and will. Timing and readiness are also essential. If you are not willing to alter your behavior and if you don't devote enough effort to your therapy, then nothing will happen.

The Green Therapies are approaches you can use to modify your behavior. They won't take the place of formal therapy, but if you give them your full attention, you will be rewarded for your efforts.

Chapter 7
Cognitive Behavior Therapy

In this therapeutic system it's the thought that counts. In fact, this theory relies heavily on the contention that how a person thinks determines how he feels and reacts. If he thinks and believes negative thoughts, his feelings and behavior will be negative. Cognitive therapy would disagree with the kid's street rhyme: "Sticks and stones will break my bones but names will never hurt me." If the names (or labels) we apply to ourselves are negative ("I'm a failure with money"), then names certainly can harm us.

A person may have developed certain ways of thinking (cognitions) very early and may not even be aware of the assumptions she is making. For example, a person who is often worried about her own competence might think: "If I don't do something perfectly, then I'm a failure." The same person might think, "I'm afraid to start a budget because I might make a mistake," or "I'll never be able to do a budget because the one I did never worked out." She would probably not know that she was thinking these negative, self-defeating thoughts, but she might find herself avoiding making budgets and getting disappointed or sad about anything to do with money. Until she is able to think more realistically, she will continue to feel overwhelmed by her belief that she is inept in certain money-management situations.

Cognitive behavior therapy helps people to see that their feelings and actions are governed by illogical arguments instead of proper deductive reasoning.

The Power of Reason

Let's use a syllogism to explain how this works. A *syllogism* consists of two propositions—a major premise and a minor premise—and a conclusion drawn from them. A well-known example is: All men are mortal; kings are men; therefore, kings are mortal.

I call the false money arguments that my clients make *sillygisms* because they begin with illogical and false major premises that guarantee a gigantic false conclusion. For example, here is one Gerald Tightwad used without knowing it. It formed an important part of the maladaptive belief system he set up for himself. His unstated argument went like this: "A lot of money hoarded away can protect me from danger (anxiety); I sense danger almost all the time; therefore, I hoard as much money as I can." Gerald knew that he was tight with money and that he felt anxious or afraid. He was, however, unaware of his major premise: "A lot of money hoarded away can protect me from danger (anxiety)." Once he realized he was making the assumption, he recognized that it was false, and that both his subsequent conclusion and the behavior he based on it were false, too.

Zora, a thirty-one-year-old unmarried woman, believed that marrying for money was the most important thing she could do. Zora's "sillygism" went like this: "Lots of money means you can get whatever you want and be happy; marrying someone who's wealthy is the only way I will ever be able to get a lot of money; therefore, I must marry an affluent man." Since Zora had not found a rich man to marry, she felt both unhappy and unsuccessful. Her irrational belief was that she had to have a great deal of money to feel secure and worthwhile.

Negative Money Attitudes

Self-defeating thoughts are characterized by self-blame, guilt, unresolved anger, and low self-esteem. They are riddled with distortions, including *overgeneralizations* (in which a single negative event is seen as a never-ending pattern of defeat) *arbitrary conclusions* (in which one thought does not follow from another), and *black or white thinking* (in which everything is all or nothing).

Here are some examples:
- I *always* lose money *all the time* (*overgeneralization*).

- Others won't like me *if* I make a lot of money and am successful (*arbitrary conclusion*).
- I'll *never* make any money, I'll *always* be broke (*overgeneralization*).
- In this world, you're *either* rich or poor (*overgeneralization, black or white thinking*).
- Having money *only leads* to problems (*arbitrary conclusion*).
- If I don't balance my budget *perfectly*, then I'm a failure (*black or white thinking*).

Other negative attitudes include:

Negative Selective Perception (in which a single negative occurrence drowns out everything else). When Marie found out that her parents bought a present for her sister that cost twenty-five dollars more than the gift she received, she was quite upset. All she could think about were the twenty-five dollars. Marie chose to disregard the times when she received things that were more costly than the items her sister received.

Faulty Labelings (in which a negative self-image defines a person's life). Mike played the stock market quite regularly. He enjoyed it and was reasonably adept at picking winners. But when his stocks went down, he couldn't brush it off as bad luck or a poor choice. Instead, he labeled himself as a failure and became extremely depressed.

Eliminating or Downplaying Positive Behavior (in which nothing is ever good enough). Susan had saved up $7,000 by the time she was twenty. She did this by judiciously putting aside whatever money she could over a period of years. When she learned one day that her friend Marcia had $8,500, her poor self-image flared: "What I've saved doesn't count; Marcia will always have more money than I have."

Overpersonalizing (in which a person takes credit or blame for things he or she has no control over). When Harold's father told him he lost money in an investment, Harold blamed himself for not warning his father to avoid that investment, even though he wasn't consulted. Harold arbitrarily made it his own fault.

Excessive Use of Commands (in which the words *should, ought,* and *must* are used excessively). One mother was plagued by the idea that she *should* give her daughter more money to spend. A grandfather gave himself a very hard time about how he *ought* to have set up a trust fund for his grandson, since his friends had done so for their grandchildren. A young woman in her thirties berated herself regularly: "I *shouldn't* spend money on myself. If I do I'm being selfish."

Jumping to Conclusions (in which the wrong conclusions are made). Joe was going to ask for a raise but as he approached his boss's office he saw Louis leaving with a confident smile. Joe concluded that Louis asked for and received a raise and that there would be no point in asking for one now.

Automatic Thoughts

People frequently are not aware of these negative attitudes and maladaptive thoughts. It's as though they were on automatic pilot; they act without understanding why they behave as they do.

In my work with clients I have helped them to become aware of these automatic thoughts so they can be typed, clarified, and analyzed. Once a person recognizes his automatic thoughts he can begin to alter their content and their effect on his behavior.

Locating the Automatic Thought

One way to find the automatic thought is to look for the connecting link. For example, a forty-two-year-old client named Marty reported that one day as he was walking down the street, he started to feel depressed. He had no idea what caused his change in mood. When I asked him to review the situation, here's what he came up with: "I was walking home from the subway when I noticed a Rolls-Royce coming down the street. By the time I got to my front door I was feeling really down."

Let's see if we can locate the automatic thought. The stimulus was seeing the expensive car; the response was feeling dejected.

With some probing we discovered the missing link: "Here I am, forty-two years old, with a good job, a home, and a nice car. There's no way in a million years I will ever earn enough money to buy a Rolls-Royce. I know it sounds silly, but in a way I feel like a failure." That relatively innocent-sounding missing thought was responsible for Marty's feelings of resentment, anger, and questionable self-worth.

How To Use Cognitive Therapy

Now that we have seen how distorted automatic thoughts can interfere with efficient financial management, we are ready to look at the how-to part of Cognitive Behavior Therapy.

The first step in Cognitive Behavior Therapy is to draw up a contractual agreement between you and the therapist (or someone who will assume responsibility for holding you to the contract) that sets out what you will do and how you will do it and a reward and penalty system to reinforce the learning process. A written contract looks like this:

> I agree to spend two hours each week trying to increase my understanding of the problems that I feel are interfering with my life—particularly my money-handling attitudes and behavior. I will also try to change my thinking and to implement the things I learn into my life to the best of my ability. Each week that I am successful, I will get to buy a new record. If I fail, I will give up my favorite TV show that week.

The rewards and penalties can include activities, objects, or sums of money. The person who holds the contract can be responsible for making sure you stick to it.

The second step is to uncover your automatic thoughts. It's often not easy to recognize these thoughts. It takes time, effort, and practice, but you should be able to do it if you're motivated. If necessary, get some professional counseling to facilitate the process.

As you catch yourself at these subliminal thoughts, write them down in a notebook. You may realize that you are thinking things like:
- I should be making more money but I never get a break.
- I'm too afraid to take chances with my money.
- I can't stand not having any money.
- It isn't fair that my colleague has more money than I do.
- There must be something wrong with me: I'm always mishandling my funds.
- By thinking about financial matters all the time, I'm harming my family.

Examine the thoughts and see them for what they are—irrational.

The third step in this process is to realize that you are not your negative thought. You and it are not one and the same. Differentiate yourself from the thought, but realize that it is having a harmful effect on you.

The fourth step is to replace your unhealthy thoughts with healthy thoughts. Read through your notebook and question your thoughts. Perhaps you wrote, "I need to have a lot of money to be happy." Ask yourself if this is really true. Do you *need* a lot of money, or do you *want* it?

Restate the "shoulds" and "musts" in your faulty thinking and beliefs. Thoughts you have to catch yourself at—such as, "I should be able to earn twice as much money, otherwise I won't feel worthwhile," or "I must have money around when a friend wants to borrow some, otherwise I feel I've rejected him"—must be challenged and altered. Positive self-messages might read: "I would like to increase or even double my earnings, but I'm not ready to do it yet. I feel good about using a plan to implement my financial goal," and "I feel good when I have extra money around to help a friend in need. But I can't always do this; sometimes I have to turn my friend down." The alteration and replacement of your internal sentences can have a major effect on the way you think about and handle money.

Step five involves changing your behavior. If you have discovered that you have been irrationally telling yourself that the only way you can feel worthwhile is to go on frequent spending binges, you need to replace these thoughts and the actions that go with them with healthy alternatives. For example, you might shop for an item that fits into your budget. If you are feeling inadequate, insecure, or not good about yourself, deal with these issues directly. Sort out the unhealthy thoughts that are keeping these feelings alive. Money should not be made the fall guy.

If you are able to improve your maladaptive thinking and correct some of the erroneous beliefs affecting the way you think about money, that's great. If not, go as far as you can, then seek out some expert counseling.

A Case History: Earl

Impaired self-image and self-esteem often create feelings of inadequacy. To uncover these unhealthy and negative thoughts, it is often necessary to dig beneath the layers.

Earl, a thirty-five-year-old successful book editor, came to see me about his anxieties. He was worried he would not have enough money to meet his needs, and he was experiencing a good deal of stress even though his job paid well and he had money saved. When I asked him to explore his fantasies, he realized that he was afraid if he ran out of money he would have to borrow from his parents or relatives or find himself out on the street. I pushed further. Well, then he would have to go to a public institution for care, and this frightened him. It soon became clear that his automatic thoughts held a litany of the horrors in store for him.

Beneath Earl's concerns about money were feelings of inadequacy, anxiety about his dependency, and tension about losing control over his own life. Once again, money had taken on the mantle of these psychological concerns and became the vehicle for neurotic behavior. Due to Earl's readiness and motivation, he began making gains as early as two months after starting his therapy.

Checklist For Cognitive Behavior Therapy

Read this list, then work through it, one item at a time, checking off each task as you complete it.

Completed

1. Complete a contract in which you agree to fulfill your therapy goals. Include in it a list of rewards and penalties. ☐
2. Practice uncovering your automatic thoughts about money and observe how you upset yourself with these thoughts. ☐
3. Write these thoughts down in a notebook. Form them into a list that you can challenge. ☐
4. Understand that your negative thoughts about money can be changed once you pin them down. Realize that they are in your mind and that you can control them. ☐
5. Challenge your mistaken beliefs and replace your irrational thoughts about money with rational ones. Consider utilizing other Green Therapies, like Thought Stopping, to assist in achieving these goals. ☐

Chapter 8
Destressing and Systematic Relaxation

As most of us know, excessive amounts of stress can add to and help to create emotional and physical ailments. Destressing and Systematic or Progressive Relaxation are therefore frequently included as part of an overall psychotherapy program. To be most effective, stress management, like money management, must be a built-in, ongoing component of a person's life.

Various approaches to relaxation, such as yoga and meditation, have been with us for a long time. These and other methods can help people reduce their unhealthy reactions to stress. Relaxation can help them avoid such reactions as spending more and more money or shopping excessively.

These relaxation skills can then be combined with Cognitive Behavior Therapy (see Chapter 7) to gain greater control of thoughts, images, and feelings. One attempt to blend relaxation with cognitive therapy is vividly referred to as *stress inoculation*: it's like using antibodies to fight off unhealthy stress.

Using Relaxation Skills

Many of my clients who are experiencing money-related anxieties and tensions find relaxation skills useful as a way of coping more effectively, especially when used in conjuction with some of the other Green Therapies. Relaxation skills are relatively easy to learn and use, but they require, once again, motivation and conviction.

In my work with Larry Gamble, for example, a destressing program was most helpful in lessening the intensity of his need to play irresponsible games with his money. I asked Larry to find a picture that induced in him a feeling of calm and peace and to look at this picture and then close his eyes and imagine it before and after doing his relaxation exercises each day. Eventually, Larry only had to look at the picture to feel relaxed. Still later, just recalling it would enable him to mentally and physically embrace the relaxed state of being he achieved during his home sessions.

Larry began his "peace-induction" work while lying down. Gradually he was able to do his exercises sitting or walking. Whenever Larry felt his anxiety level rising—particularly when he anticipated betting sums of money—he was able to "crowd out" his stressful feelings.

Using Relaxation Therapy—Getting Ready

This process works on the principle that two opposing states of feeling—relaxation and stress—cannot simultaneously maintain themselves. One has to give way to the other. There are a number of ways to reduce stress. The primary form I have used with my clients is an audiotape of progressive relaxation. You may wish to purchase such a tape, or to make one yourself.

Whether you use a tape or not, find a quiet place at home where you can practice your exercises each day for at least a half hour. Then find a picture that evokes in you a sense of calm. Most people choose scenes of nature without any people, but whatever suits your needs is fine.

When you do the exercises, lie down in a restful and comfortable position and begin with some deep breathing. Inhale and exhale slowly several times until you feel slightly light-headed. Bring to mind your peaceful picture and use your imagination to put yourself in the picture. If it's a warm outdoor scene, for example, feel the warmth and pleasantness of its atmosphere. Now you are ready to begin.

Relaxation Technique

The basic idea behind progressive relaxation is the gradual de-stressing of muscle groups from your head to your toes. You achieve this by separately tensing each muscle group, holding it in the tense state for about five seconds, and then slowly relieving the tension as you say softly to yourself, "I'm relaxing and letting go of all of my tensions." Follow the tensing and detensing of muscle groups with a couple of deep breaths and a repetition of the relaxation message.

Begin the whole procedure by tightening up every muscle in your body for a few seconds, then letting go with a big breath of relief. Feel and recognize the difference between being tense and being relaxed.

Then you begin to tighten and relax every group of muscles starting with your scalp (tense your forehead); your eyes (squint); your mouth and jaw (open your mouth); your neck and shoulders (shrug); your arms and hands (clench and push down); chest and back (tighten); your stomach (tighten, push out then in); your thighs (tighten); your legs and feet (push heels, tighten leg muscles, point toes).

I'll use the shoulders to illustrate the basic method you will use throughout your body. You can adapt these instructions for use with the other muscle groups. If you like, you can write them down, then make a tape to play while you do the exercises.

> Shrug your shoulders up as high as you can, almost as if you're going to touch your ears. Feel the tension as it builds up in your shoulders and the surrounding areas, particularly your neck. Feel the tension mount. Hold it . . . hold it . . . hold it. . . . Now, let go of the tension, let it drain away. Feel relaxed, calm. Let your relaxed shoulders become part of the body that you have already relaxed [your head and face should be already completed]. Let them blend together.
>
> Now take a couple of deep breaths. Hold them and let them go slowly. Repeat slowly to yourself: "I'm relaxing and letting go of all my tensions." Notice how your body is beginning to feel more peaceful and at ease. Observe how your tension and stress are being converted into relaxation, which is gradually taking over your whole body. Feel the difference. Feel how good it is to let the stress out of your body.
>
> Focus on your right shoulder. Tense it, shrugging it up toward your right ear. Feel the tension mounting in your neck and right shoulder. Hold it . . . hold it . . . hold it. . . . Now

relax and feel the stress draining away, leaving you with a peaceful, refreshing feeling. Take two deep breaths. As you let go, say: "I'm relaxing and letting go of all my tensions."
    Repeat the same exercise for your left shoulder and neck. Allow yourself to become loose and limp.

In doing this exercise, or any of the Green Therapies, remember to be patient and persistent. Don't expect immediate results. Change takes time.

A Case History: Harriet

Harriet had a very hard time relaxing. Everything about her was high-strung: she spoke fast, moved quickly, and had to be physically on the go all the time. Her anxiety and her blood pressure would rise whenever her twenty-five-year-old daughter called her to say she had spent money on some new clothes. Harriet's position was clear: "Why does Arlene have to buy new clothes all the time? She already has enough clothes."

Harriet got very tense when she imagined all those dollar bills—hundreds of them—flying out the window. Needless to say, her money style was very different from her daughter's. When she came to me for therapy, we began with some cognitive work and some progressive relaxation as well.

Harriet agreed she needed to reduce the stress she felt whenever her daughter spent what Harriet considered to be excessive amounts of money, but she resisted settling down to a relaxation program. We analyzed some of her hidden internal messages and found one of them to be: "I don't think these exercises will help me. I had these feelings when my daughter was younger." Harriet's reluctance to try relaxation was actually an effort to hold on to her old ways of behaving and to avoid letting go of her false thinking. Harriet finally realized her real fear was that Arlene would squander her inheritance after Harriet died. Her changed perception helped her to release her tensions and relax. She learned to respect the difference between herself and her daughter and to loosen her mental reins regarding spending. Together with other

Green Therapies, relaxation helped Harriet achieve a greater degree of inner peace. I encouraged her to build these exercises into her life so that whenever money anxieties of any kind arose she could use her relaxation exercises to help displace the unwanted and unpleasant feelings. People who become adept at relaxation are able to relieve anxiety quite readily.

Checklist for Destressing and Systematic Relaxation

Read this list, then work through it, one item at a time, checking off each task as you complete it.

Completed

1. Buy or prepare an audiotape of progressive relaxation. ☐
2. Select a peaceful scene (picture) for use with relaxation exercises. ☐
3. Designate a quiet and calm place at home to practice destressing. ☐
4. Practice the breathing exercises you will use during relaxation training. ☐
5. Listen to the complete relaxation tape prior to training. ☐
6. Gaze at the peaceful picture and start to move into it. ☐
7. Complete one full cycle of all muscle groups while listening to your tape. ☐
8. Relax for a period of about fifteen minutes following destressing session. Recall the peaceful picture. ☐
9. Repeat these steps daily until you are able to elicit a calm inner state at will. Call upon these peaceful feelings to displace tension, stress, and anxiety. Afterward, practice on a less regular basis. ☐

Chapter 9
Psychodynamics

People learn to associate money with many of their psychological needs, including their needs for status and recognition, love and intimacy, power, achievement, sexual expression, and autonomy. Our attitudes toward money, which are determined by our needs, play a major role in influencing how we choose to handle our finances—saving, spending, earning, investing, donating, and sharing.

Using psychodynamics, you can explore the assorted unconscious conflicts that are generated in you as you try to meet your needs. It is essentially an analytic technique and tries to uncover the hidden meanings and the unconscious connections of our behavior by exploring our wishes, fantasies, and dreams as well as our childhood experiences and our relationship with parents and siblings.

Applying the Psychodynamic Approach

The psychodynamic approach will help you learn why you behave in certain ways. When used in conjunction with the other Green Therapies, it will place you in a more advantageous position to effect self-change. (It is important to understand that you are not "psychoanalyzing" yourself; rather, you are using tools to increase your self-knowledge and thereby your Moneysanity.)

Step One: Your Money Psychohistory

The first step in this process is to examine your money psychohistory. From this, you will be able to formulate some hypotheses about where your money hangups came from, what needs they served, and how they were "nurtured" and continued into adulthood. Write down your answers to the following questions:

1. What is your earliest memory concerning money? How old were you? What do you actually remember? What meaning would you give to the experience?
2. When did you first become aware of the role of money in your life? What do you recall? Are they positive or negative images? Give details.
3. Were you ever taught about money? If so, what were you told? If not, how did you learn about finances? Did this lead to positive attitudes? Explain.
4. How did your mother and father view money? Did they have hangups about cash? Explain. Specifically, how did their views affect you?
5. Do you remember receiving an allowance? If so, when? Was it a comfortable experience or a hassle? Explain.
6. What money experiences do you recall during your school years, from grades one through junior high school? Include home and social experiences. What money attitudes emerged during these years? Give details.
7. What were your monetary interests during high school? Was there any shift in your attitudes toward money? Give details. Were there any changes in your family's attitudes?
8. In the years after high school and until your first full-time job, what money experiences do you recall? Give details. Have you formulated any financial plan for the next several years? If not, why not? Explain.
9. As an adult, what are your attitudes toward saving, spending, borrowing, and investing? Explain. Do you have a philosophy of money? If not, why not? Explain.
10. Do you know how your early awareness and knowledge about money matters influenced the way you handle money today? Explain.
11. Have you had or do you now have psychological conflicts about money? Give details. If yes, why do you think you have these problems? Explain as best you can.
12. How have you coped with your money hangups in the past? What changes are you prepared to make in the future? Give details.

Once you have answered these questions, you will be able to make some assumptions about the evolution of your distorted or irrational money concepts. If you find that you have conflicts about spending or saving or that you are trying to satisfy a basic human need with money, then you will have to decide how to cope more effectively.

Understanding the details and inner workings of your neurotic money habits does not mean that they will automatically disappear. But these insights, combined with other Green Therapy techniques, can be a mighty force for change.

Step Two: Analyzing Your Needs

As human beings we all have similar needs: food, clothing, and shelter are the most basic. Beyond these we also strive to feel loved, cared about, safe, free, recognized, valued, mentally stimulated, fulfilled, successful, and happy—to name a few. To attain Moneysanity, we must sort out how money relates to our needs and to untangle the connections where they are all knotted up.

Once you have completed the preliminary exercises, you should begin to keep a record of your sore spots. Record such incidents as the time you borrowed money and got upset about paying it back, the time you bought things you didn't need just because they were on sale, the time you had trouble making a decision about spending a small amount of money, the time you used money as a weapon to control people at work or at home. Note the event and describe what went on (the dynamics).

Try to understand the ways in which you are meeting your needs as an adult with methods you developed as a young person. Although the approaches may have helped you at the time, they now prevent you from being a psychologically healthy adult. They get in your way and you should work at giving them up. As you log them, observe them more closely and see the needs for which they substitute. For instance, you may learn that you spend money on people to cover your fear of losing their affection.

Step Three: Meeting Your Needs

Next, you must determine how you can meet your needs more realistically and maturely. Doing so may require risks. It can be scary but it can also be exhilarating. For example, giving up your habit of "buying affection" involves taking a chance. You will have to deal with the knowledge that people might not accept you for what you are and that your relationships rest on false premises. I have worked with many clients who have lived on a meager diet of "emotional crumbs" rather than take a chance. By doing so, they are living below the psychological poverty level.

A Case History: Carol

Since neurotic difficulties relating to money are not in fact problems of money, they can never be solved by money. It took Carol a long time to understand this. As a child she felt controlled by her parents and teachers. She felt like a servant to the authority figures in her life who seemed to be constantly demanding things and pushing her around.

She longed for the time when she would be able to conduct her life according to her own tenets rather than everyone else's. Her liberation would occur, she believed, when she had enough money to control her own life.

When she finally got out on her own and developed a successful business career, she used her money as a buffer in her social environment. She was distrustful of close relationships, which she feared would limit her freedom.

When she came to me for help, I first encouraged her to trace her attitudes toward money using the Money Psychohistory. She was then able to link her behavior with important elements in her relationship with her mother and father. She learned, among other things, that while she had been running from her parents' clutches, she had also been denying her need to be dependent.

Carol came to understand that she was repeating in her present life the defensive behavior she had developed to cope with the control exerted by her parents when she was a child. Using psychodynamics, she was helped to increase her trust of friends and others, and she began to use her money for fun rather than as a "shield" to protect her privacy and to maintain her distance from people.

Checklist for Psychodynamics

Read this list, then work through it, one item at a time, checking off each task as you complete it.

Completed

1. List your problems with money. ☐
2. Complete the money psychohistory questions. ☐
3. Make some preliminary associations between your responses and the problems you listed and draw up some hypotheses to connect your current money hangups to your early history. ☐
4. List possible neurotic meanings money might have in your life. ☐
5. Analyze ways you use money to satisfy your needs—particularly those that were unmet or partially unmet in childhood. ☐
6. Keep a notebook or a log of incidents when you use money neurotically. ☐
7. Analyze what needs you were trying to meet at these times. ☐
8. From all of this information, formulate a number of sore spots where other Green Therapies may be helpful. Set up a specific plan to remedy your money neuroses. ☐

Chapter 10
Assertive Behavior Training

In my clinical work with married couples, I have often been amazed at how creative, if not brilliant, they are at blending their neuroses. Some matches seem inspired, as, for example, the case in which the wife just happened to be compulsive about saving money and her husband just happened to be a spendthrift, the kind who runs up telephone-directory charges rather than look up numbers in the phone book. They drove each other crazy! I call this the "negative treadmill."

To rid themselves of their neurotic inclinations, all they had to do was reverse the process into a positive treadmill. By doing this, they would reinforce positive, affirmative actions, rather than their opposites. What they required to bring this about was, in part, self-assertion.

In the past, the husband had resented his wife's criticisms of how he spent his money. His response had been to rid himself of the bad feelings by acting out his hostility toward her by spending even more money, which he knew would greatly upset her. We worked on reversing this negative treadmill by employing assertiveness techniques. The husband learned to express his anger toward his wife directly by telling her how he felt. He no longer needed to behave badly with money to get back at her. She in turn was able to see how her actions had reinforced his negative feelings toward her.

The Need for Assertiveness Therapy

Many people in our society have difficulty being assertive. Assertiveness does not mean acting aggressively, but rather it is the ability to express one's feelings and opinions openly without fearing other people's reactions—particularly disapproval or disagreement. Here are some typical examples where assertiveness plays an important role. See if they apply to you.

- If a person has borrowed a sum of money and has not returned it, do you mention the matter?
- When you are short-changed in a department store, how do you handle the situation?
- Do you feel free to discuss the matter when a repair person changes an estimated fee?
- When you end up paying a larger share for groceries than your roommate, do you openly and freely discuss the cash discrepancies?
- When your date assumes it's a dutch treat and you assume he's paying for lunch, would you clarify your understanding of the financial situation?

The key elements in all these examples are standing up for yourself and expressing your rights without undue anxiety and without feeling selfish.

 Assertive Behavior Training shares with the cognitive approaches the assumption that your thoughts determine your self-image and your subsequent behavior. In Assertive Behavior Training, you change your behavior first. When you alter your behavior, you feel differently about yourself, and others do also. Joyce Spendthrift, for example, used Assertive Behavior Training in conjunction with relaxation and imagery to expand her good feelings about herself. It was important for her to learn to say no to overspending, so she wouldn't use money to quell her anxieties.

 The assertive Green Therapy teaches you how to express your concerns and rights in matters pertaining to money. Whether you are applying for a loan, asking for the return of your money, discussing financial integrity with the tax department, requesting an account of how your funds are being spent in a joint venture, or establishing fiscal equality with your mate, you can liberate yourself from nonassertive, monetarily self-defeating behaviors.

Employing Assertive Behavior Therapy

Start your assertiveness training by reviewing your money-management activities. Keep a daily record of experiences in which you should have been assertive. Next to the incident, describe how you handled it, what you did or didn't do, and what you might have done to have been more assertive.

These notes will give you a record of how you operate now. Based on this knowledge, decide how far you have to go to get to the assertiveness level you want to be at. Decide where you need assistance and list these areas in order of priority.

Once you have set up your priority list, select a practice situation. Choose one in which you have a good chance of success. For example, if you find it easier to ask for your money to be returned than to borrow cash, work on the less stressful experience first. Assertiveness tends to be its own reward and it is important to have as much success as possible.

Think about your practice situation. Recall all its nuances. Perhaps you might recall, as Andy did, receiving a commission check that was less than expected from the real-estate company he worked for. He had wanted to say something but he was concerned that he was already seen as a complainer. The amount was not great, but he felt cheated. He ended up not saying anything because he lacked the assertiveness to do so.

Andy and I worked on this incident together. Andy first reviewed all aspects of his response to the event and wrote down everything he could remember about his thoughts and reactions at the time. Next to these entries in his notes, I asked him to write down alternative responses he might have made. Following this exercise, I asked Andy to reprogram his memory by visualizing positive, affirmative steps he could have taken, and by imagining himself taking those steps.

Role Playing and Beyond

The next step in the process is to role-play a situation. In Andy's case, he did it with me in therapy. If necessary, you can ask a friend or someone you trust to help you. The element of trust is extremely important in role playing and cannot be overstressed. A high degree of trust is essential in order to feel sufficiently comfortable and free to carry out this sensitive and personal exercise. Its success depends very much on this critical factor.

In the role playing, practice saying and doing what you imagined yourself doing in the previous step. Your friend should play the other roles in the situation (see Chapter 14).

After you practice, it's time to experiment in actual situations. Monitor what you do and say and keep a record, observing where you may have failed to assert yourself. Continue the process, going back to earlier steps when necessary.

Be patient with yourself. Expect setbacks. Allow yourself to be as flexible as possible, and tell yourself it's okay to fall short of your goals at times. Be certain that your goals are realistic and attainable under the circumstances. Do it in small steps so you can achieve what you set out to do. If you find you are not making gains over a period of time after your best efforts, consider getting some professional assistance. Be at least assertive enough to get the help you might need.

A Case History: Roberta

When money is used as a weapon it can be quite difficult to assert yourself. Where Roberta was concerned, this was exactly the case.

Roberta's daughter, Sylvia, was a twenty-seven-year-old "professional student." She had talked her parents into letting her live with them by claiming not to have any money or any place to go and by pulling her "poor me, I'm a helpless little girl" routine. Her parents, and particularly her mother, were more likely candidates for the title "helpless." Roberta seemed unable to say no to her daughter. Every time Roberta felt inadequate as a parent, Sylvia turned the situation to her financial advantage.

Practicing Assertive Behavior Training with Roberta was extraordinarily difficult. In the beginning, when Sylvia asked for money, Roberta felt annoyed (although she didn't say so) and guilty. She felt that she was an inadequate mother who had failed her daughter and that she therefore "owed" her daughter. Sylvia

Assertive Behavior Training

continued to ask for money after Roberta explained all this to me. Eventually, Roberta realized that her feelings were not appropriate and she began to communicate her thoughts when Sylvia asked for money. Instead of responding to her daughter's requests for money with repressed annoyance and resurgent guilt, she was able to tell Sylvia that her requests were unreasonable and that she was quite capable of earning some money to pay for her own support. Sylvia was surprised and, in an odd sort of way, relieved that her mother was standing up for herself—finally.

Checklist for Assertive Behavior Training

Read this list, then work through it, one item at a time, checking off each task as you complete it.

Completed

1. Get into a peaceful state of mind using Destressing and Systematic Relaxation (see Chapter 8). ☐
2. Keep a daily list of incidents that require assertiveness. Describe what you did and what needs to be done to raise your level of assertiveness. (What you're doing is called establishing a "baseline.") ☐
3. Create a list of situations in order of priority in which you want to be more assertive. ☐
4. Choose a sample item of behavior to change. Hold it in your mind and recount all the nuances of the experience.
5. Reprogram the memories with positive, affirmative steps to be taken in situations that require assertive behavior. ☐
6. Role-play these situations to rehearse new ways of behaving. ☐
7. Practice assertiveness in actual situations. ☐

Chapter 11
Psychological Flashcards

In my work with clients over the years it occurred to me that people need a support-resource system nearby to reinforce their therapeutic goals. They require something that is uncomplicated, easy to carry, straightforward, and consistent—in effect, a portable mentor. Out of this realization emerged the invention of Psychological Flashcards.

This Green Therapy technique can be adapted to any situation in which you wish to change your behavior. However, before you can formulate ways to liberate your actions, you will need to use the other Green Therapies to examine your negative thought patterns and explore your psychological history. Then you need to learn how to destress and assert yourself as a way of coming to terms with your distortions about money. (These therapies are described in Chapters 7 to 10.)

Once these goals have been reached, these approaches can be written on Psychological Flashcards.

A Case History: Kathy

Kathy was a successful columnist for a magazine and money was very important to her. She was aggressively determined to make as much of it as she could; if her investments weren't going well, she worried and became moody. She wasn't aware of the rift her absorption with money was creating between her and Ian, her husband, who finally got fed up with her arrogance and preoccupation with money. He told her she was becoming suspicious and boastful. Kathy, unaware of her own actions, denied it. When Ian urged her to see a counselor, she refused: she felt insecure and threatened by the idea of actually looking at her own actions honestly. When Ian hinted that he would leave her, Kathy agreed to seek help.

It took about three months for Kathy to gain some insight into her problems, which included worrying, fluctuating moods, and anger toward Ian. She needed a way to guide her responses in a positive direction, so we developed a set of psychological flashcards.

This device is particularly useful when someone is having trouble with controlling her impulses. The cards are based on the same principles as those used by children to help them learn their multiplication tables.

Kathy and I created a list of comforting and supportive personal messages such as: "I understand what money means to me and I feel better when I use it rationally." Some of the cards also have pictures and drawings under the words to support and reinforce the relearning process. I began by telling Kathy to create a list of positive self-communication messages, which would counter the problem areas she had come to understand better: worrying, impulsiveness, fluctuating moods, and unresolved feelings about her husband. Kathy tended to think in terms of negative outcomes. I wanted her to write positive, affirmative sentences that might have come from a concerned mentor and therapist. The idea was to write as many items as she could think of; we would then eliminate the weaker entries. Here is her list:

Category	Statements
Mood	I understand what my money means to me and I feel better when I use it rationally.
Worry	My worrying is greatly reduced when I am relaxed and don't feel stressed.
Worry	Worry is a waste of my energies. I can dissolve my worries and convert them into positive actions.
Mood	When I stop being moody, through relaxation and thought stopping, I feel calmer and happier and I handle my money more effectively.
Relationship with Husband	As I come to understand my relationship with Ian, I can deal with my money-related problems better.

Kathy used these statements to help her ego. The help was available at any time of the day or night, whenever she needed it; it was always on call.

When you make your list, include several statements for each category; the statements should be positive, factual, and supportive.

Enter each item on a three-by-five index card. You may want to color code each category—for example, blue for mood, red for worry, orange for relationships. You should create six to ten statements for each category. When one of these categories causes stress, you can employ the Psychological Flashcards in addition to other Green Therapies.

Using the Psychological Flashcards

Select the set of cards that matches a stressful situation—for example, the worry set if you begin to worry. Holding the cards in the palm of your hand, read the first statement to yourself, then put the first card at the end. Then read the second, and so on until you have read all the cards. Go through the whole set two or three times until you feel the statements are becoming more and more a part of you. The sequence of the cards can be altered until you find the most effective order. And you may want to paste pictures of peaceful scenes on the backs of the cards or under the written message, to enhance the positive effects you are creating within yourself.

The Psychological Flashcards were particularly effective with Kathy. She especially needed emotional support and reassurance about her relationship with Ian, which was directly connected with her self-confidence in money matters. We spent a lot of time finding examples of Ian's care and concern. To Kathy's surprise, we came up with more positive experiences than negative ones. Gradually, during the next four months, Kathy began to understand that Ian cared for her. There were ups and downs in this process, to be sure, but the breakthrough came when she recalled a memory—long forgotten, but stimulated by her use of the Psychological Flashcards. Kathy remembered the time she came home to find her husband with a gold bracelet she had long been admiring in a jewelry-store window. He had bought it as a surprise for her.

Kathy kept a complete set of cards with her in her handbag and used them whenever needed. She used them on the subway, waiting for a dentist appointment, or sitting on a park bench. The idea was to repeat the messages routinely to herself whenever possible, as a corrective learning experience. The messages strengthened a reliable belief system and led Kathy to more affirmative and rational money-management behavior.

A Back-Up System

The Psychological Flashcards also work well as a support system to back up other Green Therapies, such as Cognitive Behavior Therapy.

The financial stress in Stephen's situation had more to do with style than with the amount of money around—although few would argue with him that it is always nice to have more cash available. Stephen's wife, Eileen, came from a background different from Stephen's: her family had large assets and she grew up with a slight case of "affluenza"—she had been bitten by the money bug. Stephen's parents, on the other hand, had suffered during the Depression and they impressed upon him the value of a dollar. Even after he had established a lucrative import-export business, the typical mentality of the "crash" victims survived in Stephen's money views and attitudes. When Eileen chose to invest their money in stocks and bonds, Stephen wanted to make more conservative money choices. When Eileen planned a fairly costly trip to visit her parents, Stephen suggested delaying the journey and reducing its duration. They squabbled on and off over how they spent their money.

Stephen wanted to loosen up his spending style and enjoy his money more. He also wanted to be able to discuss money with Eileen without fights and arguments. That was the goal he set.

He and I drew up a behavioral contract in which he agreed to approach his wife and discuss money. He agreed to talk to her at least twice a week for four weeks, for a minimum of a half hour each time, and to evaluate his progress at the end of that time. He also set up a program for himself whereby he would gradually spend more money more casually.

To reinforce the program, we worked out a rewards-and-penalties system: for each week that Stephen carried out his agreement, he allowed himself an extra half day of either golf or sailing, two of his passions. If he failed to live up to the arrangement, he gave up a full day of either activity.

Stephen wanted to be sure he could carry through on the deal he had put off so many times in the past, so after about five months we put together a set of Psychological Flashcards for him to ensure his success. Here's what Stephen wrote on his cards:

- I know Eileen's approach to money and I respect it. Although I want to change some of my money ways, I don't have to be like her.
- It's okay for me to have a money style different from Eileen's.
- I do not have to apologize, defend, or excuse my approach to spending money.
- I would like Eileen's approval but I'm not willing to be false to myself to gain it. I will tell her in a friendly manner what I'm willing to change and what is non-negotiable.
- I know that I can talk about this subject with a positive outcome. I can help bring it about and I will.
- I want to change some of my monetary behaviors but without outside pressure and because *I* believe in it.
- It feels good to be clear in my decisions to resolve our differences.

Stephen reviewed his cards regularly and carried them around with him to reinforce his efforts to change. The messages reminded him of his goals and directions and he referred to them frequently, particularly before his meetings with Eileen. He added new cards whenever he felt the need and revised or removed old ones to reflect the changes he was undergoing. For example, after Stephen told Eileen what changes he was willing to make and what was non-negotiable, he replaced that card with a new one.

In carrying out the terms of his contract, Stephen fell behind only once—in the first week. After the four weeks of his contract were up, he continued to use the cards quite regularly for two months. He found them extremely helpful, particularly when he felt doubtful or shaky.

His breakthrough came when he received a very expensive professional racing bicycle for his birthday. His initial reaction was shock and for a split second he thought about the money. Then he came through with a spontaneous outcry of joy at such a marvelous gift. He realized that he could let himself go and have fun around the spending of money without continuously bickering with his wife about money matters. The imprint of his family history and the financial attitudes and habits always remained with Stephen, but he conquered them to the extent that he felt happier and more liberated in his money psychology.

Checklist for Psychological Flashcards

Read this list, then work through it, one item at a time, checking off each task as you complete it.

Completed

1. Establish a list of items in relation to money that trouble you, for example, worry or mood changes. ☐
2. Create a list of messages to counter negative thoughts and feelings. ☐
3. Eliminate any messages that are weak or unclear. ☐
4. Write the remaining messages on three-by-five index cards. ☐
5. Practice running through the set of flashcards. ☐
6. Use the cards as needed afterward. ☐

Chapter 12
Letting Go

Perhaps one of the oldest forms of emotional healing is learning to let go. All psychological wisdom—and perhaps financial wisdom as well—pivots around the notion of giving up something in order to get something in return. For example, in a situation where one spouse is going to medical school while the other one works to support the household, the working spouse must postpone time together, personal plans for career development, or having a family in return for a financially desirable lifestyle down the road. In the area of financial investments, we certainly have to be prepared to risk money and perhaps time in our quest for greater rewards.

Emotional Baggage

Most people carry around a lot of negative emotional baggage, and it consumes a significant portion of their energy. Look around you: how many people do you know who hold grudges, anger, grievances, hatred, jealousies, desires for revenge, regrets, and hurts? This baggage can become a real problem when it weighs us down and consumes all our energy. It causes us to become emotionally exhausted and it alienates us from people by reducing our spontaneity and by interfering with our lives.

Listen to some grievances: "I lent him five dollars a month ago and he hasn't said a word since. He's probably going to try to rip me off." "Every time your mother buys presents for the children, she gets a more expensive gift for Arthur than for Cliff even though they're the same age. I think she does it on purpose to upset me." "I can't forget the fact that Aunt Min would not lend me money to rent that great apartment even though she had more than enough to lend. She always pretended I mattered to her." By holding on to these thoughts, we prevent ourselves from being emotionally free.

Blame and Forgiveness

There are two critical elements in all these thoughts: the first is blame and the second is the withholding of forgiveness. By blaming others and refusing to forgive them, we enable ourselves to adopt a poor-me attitude and thus justify our feelings. We refuse to let go because holding on gives us a sense (albeit a false one) of control over the situation.

People who need to learn to let go often don't recognize the fact. Test yourself. Do you have any of these traits:
- A strong tendency to blame and judge others.
- A desire to change others rather than accepting them the way they are.
- An overwhelming need to be right all the time.
- An unwillingness to exhibit a generosity of spirit toward others.
- A continuous focus on the past, which keeps you from developing and growing.

Accepting and Forgiving

The major elements in Letting Go are accepting and forgiving. Accepting others as they are rather than blaming or condemning them does not necessarily mean approving of them or their actions, or wanting to associate with them; it means *not trying to change them*. I find that this is one of the biggest problems married couples face. Forgiving others and letting the past go does not necessarily mean that you accept or approve of another person's behavior, but that you are willing to free yourself from the destructive process of bearing grudges and keeping wounds open. If you do not feel you want to associate with the person, then go your different ways, but first liberate your feelings.

A Case History: Irving

Irving is someone who has never learned to let go. He came to see me because an episode that occurred four and a half years ago was still making him unhappy. Murray, who at the time was Irving's partner in a catering business, was put in the awkward position of having to make a momentous business decision while Irving was on holiday in Europe.

The decision Murray made turned out to be the wrong one. It cost them many thousands of dollars—$65,000, to be exact. Although it was an honest error and the company was sufficiently solvent to work the debt off, Irving was so angry that he wouldn't talk to Murray. Eventually the mishap led to the dissolution of the company.

Irving held on to his anger like a Gila monster—the venomous lizard found in Arizona and New Mexico, which reportedly doesn't let go once it bites its victims. It almost seemed as if, at times anyway, he nurtured his hostility toward Murray.

Irving thought he was upset because of the lost money, when in fact his continuous high level of hostility was a cover-up for his fear of being penniless. He expressed rage toward Murray because it was convenient to attack Murray rather than to explore and discover his own psychodynamics. Irving dreaded the possibility of becoming a pauper, and although this was an extremely remote prospect, the loss of a large sum of money was enough to threaten his sense of safety. It was Murray's fault, and that was that.

Using Letting Go Therapy

My work with Irving was difficult indeed. The trouble was not with the technique of Letting Go, which is actually quite simple, but with Irving's attitude.

To begin with, Irving and I worked on relaxation and destressing techniques. After about five weeks, he began to show some positive signs. Gradually he began to feel some positive results from relaxation training, and this encouraged him to go further.

Over many years, Irving had grown used to trying to change others, to get them to do things his way. He always got frustrated with them when they failed to conform. Now he had to learn to change the old patterns; he had to learn to let go.

Letting Go can be accomplished through the imagination, through the active use of inner imagery. Here's what we did. First, Irving wrote an autobiographical sketch three or four pages in length and noted times in his life when forgiving or accepting others was an issue. He then drew up a list of these episodes from the least to the most upsetting.

Then, beginning with the first item on the list (the least anger-provoking), Irving wrote a description of the incident in a notebook, recalling the details as well as he could. Following this, he went through a relaxation session to bring himself to a peaceful state.

Working through all these stages—with many setbacks and delays—took Irving seven months. We then began working through the episodes Irving had described, beginning with item one, which was an incident that took place when Irving was eleven. His father had promised him five dollars for a day's work cleaning up debris around the house. His father forgot to give him the money and Irving reminded him. Two days passed, during which time Irving got into trouble with some other children at school. When his father found out, he told Irving to forget about the five dollars. Irving was angry and resentful, and had not yet forgiven his father for what he saw as an unjust decision.

In order to help Irving accept and forgive his father, we went through an exercise that is the prototype for all Letting Go exercises. After completing the relaxation session, Irving was instructed to recall the episode with his father in detail. He then imagined his father sitting opposite him and he told his father about his hurt and his anger and the grudges he bore him. Following this, he imagined both sides of a conversation in which he told his father that he forgave him for what happened and promised to let go of the residue of negative feelings. Irving conjured up this scene as many times as necessary until he had achieved the goal of letting go.

Irving proceeded to follow the same exercise with successive items on his list until he reached one of the hardest ones—forgiving his ex-partner, Murray. When our therapy sessions ended, almost a year after they began, Irving successfully let go of his earlier emotions, but he kept up the therapy, which was becoming a very rewarding experience for him.

Checklist For Letting Go

Read this list, then work through it, one item at a time, checking off each task as you complete it.

Completed

1. Write an autobiographical sketch, three to four pages long. Pick out problem areas—for example blaming and fault-finding, holding grudges, unwillingness to forgive and let go of the past—particularly as they relate to money handling. ☐
2. Make a list of items ranging from the one that arouses the fewest negative feelings to the one that arouses the most. ☐
3. Prepare for Letting Go exercises by completing a session of relaxation training before each new item. ☐
4. Select the first item on the list (the least troublesome) and mentally recreate the "unfinished" episode, recalling in detail what occurred. ☐
5. In your imagination, create a dialogue about the issues you are still holding on to. State as succinctly as possible what you want to express about the experience. ☐
6. At the conclusion of the dialogue, affirm your decision to forgive the other person for the grievance and start to let go (give up) the past. Repeat as needed. ☐
7. Continue the process with each new item, repeating each enough times until you achieve the goal of self-liberation. ☐
8. Affirm the value of this procedure by applying what you have learned to your present experience. ☐

Chapter 13
Thought Stopping

Thought control, when practiced by governments, represents a significant loss of freedom. When it is properly utilized to rid people of negative money attitudes, it leads to increased personal freedom.

Thought control or thought stopping is a behavioral technique that can be used to combat obsessive and worrisome financial ruminations. There are lots of different thoughts you might want to control, for example, thinking you always pay more than anyone else for the same item, thinking you can't afford to buy certain things when there is more than enough money around, or thinking you have never saved enough money.

It is important to master your thoughts because your feelings and your actions are all directly linked to your thinking. For instance, if you tell yourself (*thought*) that money is the only thing you can depend on, then you will feel insecure (*feeling*) without it and you will drive yourself (*action*) to produce more and more of it in an attempt to stay ahead of your mounting anxieties. In this way, your thoughts could cause you to lose control over your life.

A Case History: Janet

When Janet went shopping for her family, she felt fine, no matter what the occasion. But whenever she wanted to buy herself something—particularly if it was expensive—she experienced a growing sense of malaise followed by self-doubt and feelings of guilt. She was able to spend money freely on others, but only very sparingly on herself.

When Janet and I examined her thoughts, we found that she told herself that she had more than enough things and that she didn't need to add to her supply. She felt she was not worthy of expensive items, that she didn't deserve them. To eliminate her symptoms we employed a strategy called Thought Stopping.

All of us learn over the years to condense our experiences and to attach an emotional label to them: sadness, worry, self-hatred, guilt. We do this on automatic pilot, without realizing we're doing it. When Janet got the urge to buy something fancy for herself, she got depressed. The depression reinforced her negative feelings about herself and encouraged them to remain.

Using Thought-Stopping Techniques

The object of Thought Stopping is to reverse these processes, to stop rerunning past negative tapes and negative ruminations. Basically, you learn to train yourself to keep the thought away—to starve it out by not feeding it.

This is done by replacing one crop of negative thoughts with another crop of positive and strong thoughts. You must begin by creating a list of positive and pleasurable images, things like watching the sun come up on a beach in the Caribbean, making love under a waterfall in a remote mountain range in South America, taking a gondola ride in Venice, having an intimate dinner on the Left Bank in Paris, riding on the back of a hay wagon in July on a farm in Kansas.

As soon as you have composed your list, you are ready to begin. Now call forth one of your persistent negative thoughts. (For example, Janet chose the thought that she didn't deserve an expensive present.) The instant this notion enters your mind, but before it grows at all, introduce one of the images from your list of positive thoughts. Go right into it, fully and completely conjuring up the vision. The object is to preoccupy yourself totally with the new thought and to displace the offensive thought. While undergoing this thought transformation, start practicing new ways of behaving. Janet, for example, began purchasing things of greater value for herself.

Keeping the Old Thoughts Out

If the old hurtful thoughts recur, attack them by yelling, "Stop"—out loud if possible. Other shocks to dispel the negative thoughts could be clapping your hands, hitting a desk, or my favorite—snapping a rubber band on your wrist. However you achieve it, the object is to scare the hell out of the thoughtless thought and make it beat a hasty retreat. Think of them as uninvited, intruder thoughts that you are telling to leave.

You can measure your success by recording the amount of time your preoccupying thoughts take up and how frequently they occur. Note how long they last before you can start the technique, how long they stay once you have begun it. The goal is to reduce the amount of time spent thinking your negative thoughts.

A Case History: Neal

Neal had some pretty disquieting thoughts to quell that went back to his childhood in the tough area of a big city. He had been traumatized before he was a teenager on countless occasions by hostile older males "asking" him for money. He was threatened by these incidents even though he was never assaulted. He remembers one episode with humiliation and impotent rage. His would-be assailant had demanded five dollars, and Neal had given him his wallet, hoping desperately that the other kid would just take the amount he said he wanted. Instead he took all his cash and the wallet, leaving Neal feeling angry and foolish.

From these experiences, Neal developed an exaggerated fear of losing money or having it stolen and he went to extreme lengths to prevent such a happening. Money had become a symbol of apprehension.

Neal's counseling involved a variety of Green Therapies, including Thought Stopping. Over a period of two months Neal worked on creating a list of pleasurable and positive images to replace his fearful negative ones. To "starve" his thoughts rather than "feed" them, Neal drew up a list of items personally satisfying to him: visiting an art museum in Paris, watching his ten favorite movies, attending a two-hour presentation by Woody Allen of his great comedy routines, going to the three most famous concerts in Europe in August, and having a sumptuous dinner on a beach in southern France.

Whenever Neal had a negative thought, he stopped it and replaced it with one from his list of satisfying thoughts. For example, if he began to worry that something was going to happen to his money, he would immediately snap the rubber band on his wrist. He would also picture a favorite image from his list. With time, he became quite agile at making these thought switches. In this way, thought stopping—as well as other approaches—helped Neal to make substantial gains.

Checklist For Thought Stopping

Read this list, then work through it, one item at a time, checking off each task as you complete it.

Completed

1. Practice systematic relaxation exercises to gain an overall feeling of ease. ☐
2. Create a list of the most pleasurable and positive scenes, events, places, or feelings you can think of. ☐
3. Call forth a persistent negative thought. Before it can fully start, replace it with an item from your list. ☐
4. Try other methods of Thought Stopping, such as saying "Stop" to yourself, clapping your hands, or snapping a rubber band on your wrist. ☐
5. Continue to practice your thought stopping.

Chapter 14
Mini Green Therapies

In my practice, I have often advised my clients to make use of "mini green therapies." These exercises can be used separately or in association with the Green Therapies, and they are:
- Affirmations;
- Guided Imagery;
- Looking-Forward Calendar;
- Photograph Identification;
- Role-Playing;
- Tell-a-Tape;
- Creating Your Own Dictionary.

Affirmations

Affirmations are positive statements you say to yourself—out loud, silently, or by writing them—to build up your self-esteem and revise your negative money attitudes. You should use affirmations whenever you need additional help in your battle with a money problem or a negative money thought.

To begin your affirmation exercise, list your negative money thoughts. Then, opposite each thought, write a corresponding positive one. For example:

Negative Money Notion	*Affirmation*
Borrowing frightens me. I can't get myself to do it.	I'm a sensible mature person. I will approach the subject of borrowing rationally and achieve my goal.
Budgets fluster me. I don't think I can organize one.	Budgets are logical, organized money plans. I will strengthen my organizational skills and master the budget.

I sometimes have a tendency to overspend and I cover my debts with credit cards. It's a bad habit.	I have decided that I don't like how I feel when I spend too much. I am motivated to change and I will.
Paying taxes makes me angry. Even though I see some of the benefits, I have a very hard time parting with money to pay income taxes.	I will work out exactly what discretionary money I have from my budget and focus on that and not on what I can't control—like paying my income taxes.
I'm preoccupied with amassing money and I can't seem to help it.	I have decided that this tendency is interfering with my life. I am motivated to change it for good. I will change it.

Convert the negative money notions that float through your mind into positive, goal-directed statements. Practice repeating the affirmations several times a day until you feel more positive about the particular problem you are working on.

This exercise, although simple, can serve as an important and worthwhile supplement to other helpful methods for change.

Guided Imagery

Guided Imagery is a process that takes place in the imagination. It is a helpful way to rehearse for change by allowing yourself to imagine fulfilling or completing a planned money action, such as writing your will, shopping less, asking for a loan, dealing with your income-tax anxiety, or loosening up your tight money strings.

First you single out something you want to do. Then you practice the destressing and systematic relaxation therapies. Following this—and in a peaceful state of mind—you sit or lie back and imagine yourself going through whatever it is you want to accomplish.

For example, if the pursuit of bargains has gotten out of control, you might imagine yourself going to a store and buying something not on sale or not purchasing anything at all—despite the temptation.

Create your own scenarios to fit your goals. The exercise must be done sincerely, earnestly, and repeatedly—together with the other approaches—in order to be effective.

Looking-Forward Calendar

The Looking-Forward Calendar is an emotional support device that can be quite effective despite its simplicity. It is based on the realization that people often forget to be nice to themselves, and it involves building in to your ongoing schedule activities that are life-enhancing and rewarding. These activities might involve the use of your financial resources for fun and perhaps even profit.

Obtain a large desk-size calendar with big blank squares for each day. Starting at least two or three weeks ahead, write in specific activities on particular dates. Include some enjoyable money-oriented activities, such as buying things for yourself or for others (in a noncompulsive manner, of course), or taking someone out for dinner and not worrying about the expense.

Be creative, but also be sure to relate the activities to your goals. Use the Looking-Forward Calendar together with the other Green Therapies.

Photograph Identification

This procedure is sometimes used as an adjunct to or as part of Psychodynamics. By carefully examining the photos taken during our growing-up years, we are sometimes able to get some insights into the origin of our money attitudes. The photographs act as a stimulus to bring back early associations about our family relationships.

While looking at old photographs, pay particular attention to such guiding signs as the arrangement of the people in the photograph. Who is in it? How close are the individuals physically? What were their expressions? What emotional tone did they seem to show? What is your emotional reaction to the picture? What does it remind you of? Did you feel left out? Does it remind you of how you would have liked things to have been different?

Now consider how these various reactions and responses relate to the development of your money attitudes and thinking. These findings may facilitate your work on your money problems.

Role Playing

Role playing is a long-established counseling procedure. It allows for the expression and ventilation of feelings and it serves as a kind of rehearsal for real events or as a way of acting out past episodes.

The object can be to practice acting in ways you find difficult. For example, you might pretend you were speaking to a bank manager, a loans officer, or an insurance salesperson.

This technique can also be used to pretend you are talking to a parent with whom money matters were emotionally embroiled in the past. For example, you might pretend you were talking to your mother about how she bought you things instead of spending time with you, or to your father about the effects of his stinginess.

It's probably a good idea to begin a role-playing session with destressing and relaxation. Then place two chairs opposite one another and begin your dialogue, making up both sides of the conversation. You may feel odd or mechanical at first, but you'll be surprised how useful this procedure can be if you stick with it. If you wish—and it's feasible—ask someone you trust to play the other role.

An exciting variation of this approach is to arrange a role-playing situation between you and your money. Ask your money what it wants, how it likes to be spent, what special meanings it has, what makes it comfortable or uncomfortable, and similar provocative questions. Think about how your money would reply, then analyze the contributions this information can make to your understanding of how you think about money.

Tell-a-Tape

This approach uses the money psychohistory questions described in Chapter 9 on Psychodynamics, but with an important difference: you tape-record your replies. Instead of writing down your answers, you talk about the issues openly and spontaneously while the tape recorder is on. This gives you the opportunity to listen to yourself several times, so that you can pick out important clues to your feelings about money.

For example, when you respond to the question, "What is your earliest memory concerning money?" you should listen for your tone of voice (high or low), the quality of the reply (decisive or uncertain), the mood (happy or distressed), and other features such as the degree of spontaneity, resistance, or reluctance in the reply, and emotions associated with the experience (anger, fear, joy, unhappiness). Analyze the content each time you replay the tape and combine the new information with your written answers to the questions. This will enhance your self-understanding regarding your money attitudes.

Adapt the Tell-a-Tape method to other Green Therapies to increase your insights.

Creating Your Own Dictionary

This is a useful technique to increase mutual understanding about money matters. To "create your own dictionary," begin by writing down your personal definitions for such terms as: "enough money matters. To create your own dictionary, begin by writment," "miser," and "overspender." Add similar words and phrases as you go along. Then, ask your spouse (or any other person with whom you share financial responsibility) to do the same thing. Do not discuss the words beforehand.

After you have both completed your lists, exchange them and read them together. Review the similarities and differences of the meanings the words have for each of you. Discuss your discrepancies and reduce any misunderstandings. This method will ensure that when one person uses monetary terms and expressions, the other person will know exactly what is meant.

PART III
Money Stress of Everyday Life

To conquer the money stresses of everyday life, you must successfully deal with your psychological attitudes toward money as well as with your financial goals. The following chapters are, therefore, divided into two parts: the first emphasizes the behavioral aspects and the second the pragmatic considerations.

To maximize your money management skills, begin by evolving an overall financial master plan. Then tailor your individual money decisions to fit this master plan. If, for example, you need to borrow funds, do so in accord with the principles of your master plan.

Your plan should ideally involve short- and long-range goals. Your goals might include establishing a regular savings program, paying off debts, reducing income taxes, allocating funds for emergencies, maintaining the style of life you prefer or improving your standard of living, creating a "special expenses" fund, increasing your yearly net worth, and planning for retirement.

To implement these aims, it is essential to keep accurate ongoing financial records. These should include a record of money spent and money earned, statements of your present net worth, budget worksheets, insurance information, complete tax data and copies of old returns, details about your debts, and a complete picture of your investments.

The second part in each of the following chapters is designed to stimulate your thinking. To do a full and proper job in these areas, you must also be willing to keep yourself up to date. Read the financial or business section of your newspaper, find yourself a good professional advisor, and read books and other materials on the subject.

Chapter 15
The Stress of Budgeting and Life Planning

Money directly affects almost every area of our lives: getting it, borrowing it, lending it, spending it, saving it, and investing it. The average wage earner in North America can expect, during the course of a lifetime, to spend about eighty-five thousand hours working for a living. During that time it's estimated that an average high-school graduate will earn almost a million dollars. (These figures will vary, of course, with earning capacity and the vagaries of inflation.)

If we spend so much of our lives gathering and disposing of our financial resources, and if money influences so much of our existence, why then do so many of us refuse to handle it more efficiently? Most of us conduct our financial affairs like a crapshoot, leaving the outcome to chance. We find ourselves saying things like: "Oh, I know more or less how I spent my earnings last month and what was left over, I think."

Accounting for our family's finances should be part of our overall planning. Without organizing principles in our lives, we would have nothing but chaos. Drawing up a budget, therefore, is one of the important guidelines for running our lives meaningfully.

There seems, however, to be a list of objections to budgets as long as your arm. People have come up with all kinds of arguments as to why budgets are not for them. For example: they are too constricting; they limit spontaneity; they are boring; they create drudgery; they are too complicated; they are hard to follow; they lead to family feuds and disagreements; they probably don't even work.

Many people see a budget as a straitjacket that robs them of control and spontaneity. The truth is that a budget provides psychological strength and potential peace of mind by giving us a tool for much greater control over our lives. It should help to eliminate money anxieties and replace them with money enjoyment. A spending plan can do away with the "buy now, worry later" syndrome that affects many people. All a budget really does is help you decide how you're going to divide up what you do have without trying to give away what you don't have.

Organizing your personal monetary life will give you a sense of control. It is a psychological tool as well as a financial one.

Choosing a Budget

Budgets, like diets and exercise plans, require long-term commitments. Sticking to a budget for only two months does no more than sticking to a diet or exercise plan for a short period.

The program you choose must also comfortably fit your personality type. A budget is an outline of how you plan to spend your life. Its content and priorities relate directly to the values, beliefs, and attitudes you hold, even if you are not fully aware of all these things yourself. To be wiser about your money you must, therefore, know yourself. Self-knowledge is of the essence.

It is important to remember that a budget will not reform you. You cannot expect a budget to change the kind of person you are. Don't set up unrealistic expectations. For example, if you love to eat out, don't cut restaurant meals out of your spending plan. Cut them down, if you wish, but don't cut them out.

A Case History: Lillian and Herbert

The question of who controls the family budget is a major factor in the breakup of many marriages. It's fascinating to note that there is nothing new about these conflicts. The famous seventeenth-century English diarist Samuel Pepys relates this personal story:

> I and my wife went up to her closet to examine her kitchen
> accounts, and there I took occasion to fall out with her, for

buying a laced handkerchief pinner without my leave. From this we began both to be angry, and so continued to bed.

A more contemporary couple, Lillian and Herbert, used money as weapons in their arguments with each other. Herbert was a career soldier and Lillian a librarian and mother to their four daughters.

Lillian resented her husband's control over their cash supply. He would hand out "goodies" much as the army gave out allocations to the troops. Except that if she (or the girls) weren't "good," they wouldn't get their allotment. In that way Herbert was able to wound them with deadly accuracy.

One of their many arguments about money occurred after Lillian had asked for a set of pretty chinaware and Herbert had turned her down, saying that they couldn't spare the money. Eventually, Lillian bought the dishes with money she earned from small sewing jobs and from part-time library work. Herbert was enraged that she would do such a thing on her own without consulting him.

Arguments like this one and the fact that Herbert had always refused to establish a mutually agreed-upon budget formed the basis of an all-out war and led to their eventual divorce.

Let's take a closer look at what went on, starting with their family backgrounds.

Lillian's father had behaved like a martinet but she had loved him dearly. She always wanted to be on his good side since, during the rare times when she was, he showed her some open affection. On the surface she was a passive and conforming child, but underneath she felt resentment and ill will toward her father, which became generalized to other men.

Herbert's family was less rigidly controlled than Lillian's, but they also had fewer financial resources. As a result, the family was constantly concerned about financial security, and Herbert grew up feeling he had to be extra-vigilant about monetary matters. When he got hold of some funds, he clutched them tightly because he didn't know when more funds would come his way.

Lillian chose Herbert, in part, because he reminded her of her father. She set out, as so many of us do with our spouses, to reform him. She was going to be successful with Herbert in a way she never was with her father—or so she thought. One of the single most significant factors in driving people apart is the determination of one to change the other. This operation is invariably doomed to failure, as Lillian discovered for herself.

My efforts with this couple were directed at getting them to see that they were obeying some unwritten, unstated, internal edicts. They were on automatic pilot, playing out in contemporary terms the scripts of their earlier lives. Herbert didn't want to work out a joint budget; he wanted to manage the finances in his own way. Lillian found this tyranny to be reminiscent of her father.

It is impossible to know whether joint financial planning at an earlier date would have saved their marriage. A budget certainly would have represented more than a financial plan: it would have been a joint compromise on how they chose to relate. It would have symbolized a form of peace settlement between them. Their failure to reach an accord had far-reaching effects in other areas of their lives and it produced a serious rift between them.

As they drifted away from each other, I worked with them as separate individuals to strengthen their healthier sides and to teach them to avoid repeating their neurotic money patterns. Budgeting and life planning were directly relevant to success.

In a sense, Lillian and Herbert had been living without a center of control in their lives; this led to chaos. Anyone would be afraid of such an outcome. Feeling out of control is one of the scariest human experiences. People who have been pushed beyond their limits and have lost control over their lives sometimes become mentally ill. To a lesser extent, but in much the same way, not having a financial plan in our lives also leaves us in a rudderless state.

Budgets Reflect Our Lifestyles

The way we choose to spend money says a lot about the kind of people we are. Even people who grew up in the same family can be quite different in this regard. Let me give you an example.

Barbara and Amanda were sisters—although if you looked at their attitudes toward buying things you wouldn't think they had been raised in the same town by the same middle-class family according to the same child-rearing methods.

Thirty-two-year-old Barbara loved to spend the money she earned as a successful freelance writer. She enjoyed buying fashionable clothes, books, and records, and was willing to put up with a modest apartment if she could indulge her other needs.

Amanda, at twenty-nine, saw nothing wrong with sewing her own clothes and remodeling good used outfits. It wasn't that she couldn't afford new clothes; she was doing very well in a small retail business, and she managed her money conservatively. She simply preferred to spend her money on other things, like furniture and decorations for her apartment.

Barbara's and Amanda's different budget sheets reflected the differences in their tastes. They could no more swap sheets than they could live each other's lives. Both sisters used a budget to attain a sense of balance in their lives.

Getting the Most for Your Money

The way you set up your budget, what you leave in, and what you omit are directly related to your system of values. For example, if you believe that education is important or that a certain standard of living is essential for happiness, your budget will or should reflect these priorities.

Therefore, the first thing you have to do is become aware of what is and is not important to you, what values and beliefs you maintain. The basic question is: why are you earning money?

Some people's answers will be the obvious ones; but some are surprising. Alan, for example, gave a thoughtful reply: "I'm working to earn money so I won't have to be dependent on others." Jane's response was, "I'm deathly afraid of poverty. My family went through some terrible financial times. When I was young we were on the dole. I swore then I would always have money so that I wouldn't be humiliated." Douglas's reply was: "When I wasn't working and receiving a regular salary I felt and was treated like a nonperson or a leper. My self-esteem sank like a torpedoed submarine, and I was ostracized subtly by some of my former colleagues."

Presumably, we all want the good life for ourselves, but each of us has a different definition of what that life entails. To achieve it, we must know what we value and what we want out of life.

Perhaps now is a good time to ask ourselves some pertinent questions.

Money-Value Analysis Quiz

1. Why are you working and earning money? (Give reasons beyond the basics of survival.)
2. What do you want out of life? Are you getting it? How does or could money help you to get it?
3. What is the meaning and purpose of your life? Are you achieving it? How does or could money help you reach it?
4. Are you satisfied with your life? How does money fit into it?
5. Do you have long- and short-term life goals? What are they? What role does money play in achieving them?
6. What do you think the connection is between money and happiness?
7. Think about the relationship between your values and your money. Give some specific personal examples of how your values affect how you think about and handle money.
8. On the basis of the answers to the previous questions, what goals do you have that money can help you achieve?
9. How much money do you need to attain your short- and long-term goals?
10. Do you have fears, superstitions, or worries about money? What are they?
11. How do you feel about sharing money with your spouse and children? Do you prefer separate accounts or joint accounts? How do you decide how much allowance your children receive?

12. Who makes what money decisions in your family? Which decisions are made jointly? Which individually? Which in consultation with another?
13. Does the amount of money your family had (or didn't have) when you were a child affect your present attitudes? How?
14. What do you want to teach your children about money? How do you develop these attitudes in your children? What part do allowances and part-time jobs play?
15. How much money are you comfortable owing to others (credit cards, loans, mortgages, and so on)?
16. What do you like to do for fun? How much does it cost?
17. Do you enjoy spending money on others? Do you do it to buy their admiration and affection?

Once you have answered the questions, review your responses to detect trends, patterns, and tendencies in your money values. Summarize your responses under the following headings:
- the purpose and direction of your life;
- the role of money in your life;
- money and relationships.

Compare your answers with those of your spouse or partner if you have one. See if there are basic differences and if you can diminish them. Keep your findings in mind as you read the rest of this chapter. Each increase in self-awareness leads you closer to Moneysanity.

Knowing Yourself

Knowing what your beliefs, values, and attitudes are regarding questions about money will increase your self-knowledge and help you to use money more intelligently. If, for example, you hate to borrow, you might never allow yourself to take out a loan, even when it's in your best interest to do so (in order to make an investment, for example). By examining your attitudes, however, you might realize that some of your views about the wisdom of borrowing and its mechanics are quite outdated. They may be based on your parents' attitudes, which may not be applicable to our times. Perhaps this attitude should be challenged and changed. The important question may not be to borrow or not to borrow, but rather: are you a sane borrower?

What about your feelings about the place of fun and games in your budget? Some people think they can't afford good times or indulgences because they're saving up for their futures. Others believe that life is too unpredictable to make plans. They'd rather do things now. What is your position? How does it affect your spending plan?

Budgetitis and How to Cure It

Some people who have trouble with their budgets get irritated and inflamed. This may lead to *budgetitis*, or aggravation of the spending program. It comes about through direct blows to the money ego and results in confusion, monetary headaches, inflammation of the joints (joint accounts, joint relationships, joint stocks), and generally sore feelings.

To avoid losing your balance from this condition, it's essential to know where you stand. Make a clear statement to yourself. Almost everyone wants to be financially fit, but a large proportion of us do not exercise our options. We resist the money cure: a sound budget in a healthy life plan. How can *you* overcome your resistance to setting up and following a budget?

If you have resisted making a budget or if you have felt frustrated or a bit of a failure in bringing off a workable budget, maybe some of the Green Therapies could help you. Decide which of the symptoms listed in the left-hand column best describes you. The middle column lists Green Therapies (Chapters 7 to 11) you might try for the Payoff described on the right.

Curing Your Budget Headaches

Symptom	Green Therapy	Payoff
If you feel the task is overwhelming, try:	Assertiveness Behavior Training Destressing and Systematic Relaxation Cognitive Behavior Therapy Affirmations Psychological Flashcards	You will be able to structure the tasks in small steps and feel a greater sense of self-mastery.
If you suffer from insufficient interest and motivation, try:	Affirmations Thought Stopping Psychological Flashcards Cognitive Behavior Therapy Assertive Behavior Training	You will clarify your goals and purposes. This will result in renewed interest and the freeing up of energies.
If you are afraid of failing to manage your funds, try:	Cognitive Behavior Therapy Destressing and Systematic Relaxation Assertive Behavior Training Affirmations Thought Stopping	You will be able to displace fear and raise the level of your self-confidence.

(continued on next page)

Symptom	Green Therapy	Payoff
If you lack the conviction to manage your money by using a budget, try:	Thought Stopping Assertiveness Behavior Training Affirmations Psychological Flashcards	You will be increasingly able to stand up to the task.
If you proscrastinate, try:	Affirmations Thought Stopping Cognitive Behavior Therapy Assertiveness Behavior Training	You will sharpen your focus and resolution to complete tasks with definable time limits.

After carefully going through and practicing the appropriate Green Therapies, turn to the next section, The How of Budgeting, for specific help on how to actually go about setting up a budget. You should now be more free to accomplish the task at hand.

The How of Budgeting

Robert Benchley once said: "The advantage of keeping family accounts is clear. If you do not keep them, you are uneasily aware of the fact that you are spending more than you are earning. If you do keep them, you know it." As always, humor reminds us of the threads of our common experiences. Not only do we get into trouble spending more than we earn, but we all frequently end up spending more than we have—a pretty amazing trick!

Freedom is a wonderful thing—nobody can tell you what to spend your money on or how much to spend. Only you can do that.

Your Budget

Before you can decide how things should be, find out how bad they are. Begin by figuring out exactly what you earn and what you spend.

Earnings

List, to the nickel, exactly how much you earn after taxes each month from all sources, including salary, bonuses, interest, dividends, and so on. Now list the earnings of whoever else is sharing your budget: spouse, child, lover. Write the total on a piece of paper and stare at it for a while. Are you impressed, depressed, or "other"? It's just as they used to say at the end of the cartoons: "That's all, folks!" Right now, that's all there is; there ain't no more.

After you've come to accept the fact that this sum is all that keeps you and yours from the poorhouse, let's get a closer look at how you have been misspending it. First, calculate what you spend on daily and weekly expenses.

Daily and Weekly Expenses

Write down what you spend each day on ordinary items: the newspaper you buy on the way to work, your carfare, the coffee and muffin you have at coffee break, afternoon snacks, cigarettes, lunch, parking and tolls. Figure out what you spend on the average day and write the amounts next to the items.

Now do the same for the other members of your family. Figure out how much you all spend in a week. Now add the weekly expenses: groceries, cleaning, babysitting, household help, entertainment, and so on.

Knowing what you spend for seven days isn't enough. You must add up your monthly expenses. Do it now.

Monthly Expenses

Housing: rent or mortgage, property tax, water, gas, oil, electricity, telephone, cable television, and home maintenance. Transportation: gas, car maintenance, car payments, parking, public transportation, and taxis.

Child Care: day care, education fees, transportation.

Special Financial Obligations: alimony, child support, installment payments (including all credit cards), gifts, contributions and charities, tax payments, charge accounts, legal fees, accountant fees, pet care.

Now add up your yearly expenses.

Yearly Expenses

Savings and Security: insurance (life, disability, health and accident, car), pensions, bank savings, annuities, government tax-deferment plans for retirement, savings, bonds, and investments.

Personal Expenses: vacations, club memberships, dues, education.

Now work out what you spend each month on weekly, monthly, and yearly expenses and subtract the amount from your total monthly financial resources. (Is there something wrong? Why are you in a state of shock?)

Okay, now that you know what you are spending, it's time to decide what it *ought* to be. So let's change it. It's time to start your budget.

Take the Money-Value Analysis Quiz on page 114 (or review your answers if you have already taken it), to give yourself some ideas about how you want to live your life, how your values fit in, and what your priorities are. Now consider each item on your monthly expense sheet. Review your current expenses and decide if there is any room to cut back. Now, on a chart like the one on pages 121-122, write down what you would realistically like to spend. Do this for each item, add up the total and cross your fingers. If the total is less than you make, all you have to do is stick to your good intentions.

Don't let my levity mislead you. Budgets are for real. They actually do make an important and valuable contribution to organizing your financial life. Just because most people don't use them is no reason for you not to.

Expenditures

Use this budget to figure out what you would like to spend your money on. Not all the items will apply to you, and you may have expenses not covered here, but this list will give you guidelines to follow.

	Monthly	Yearly
Home		
Rent or mortgage payments		
Heat		
Electricity		
Water		
Telephone		
Cable TV		
Domestic help		
Maintenance and decorating		
Appliance repair and replacement		
Other		
Food		
Household groceries		
Eating out		
Personal Care		
Clothing		
Laundry and dry cleaning		
Hairdresser or barber		
Personal spending money		
Other		
Medical		
Health plan		
Dental		
Optician and glasses		
Medicine		
Other		
Transportation		
Public transit		
Gas and oil		
Car maintenance		
Car license		
Taxis		
Car payments		
Other		

Children
Day care
School fees
Allowances
Babysitter

Discretionary
Entertainment
Vacations
Hobbies
Special occasions (birthdays, etc.)
Donations and charity
Gifts
Liquor and tobacco
Club fees
Recreation

Taxes
Income tax
Property tax
Other

Debt Repayment
Loan payments

Savings
Regular
Retirement
Children's education
Other

Insurance
Car
Home
Life
Other

The Stress of Budgeting and Life Planning

Here are some tips to keep your budget from squeezing you too tightly.

Tip 1: Limit your credit buying. It knocks the hell out of healthy budgets. Whenever possible, leave your credit card at home. If you see something you need, you can always go back tomorrow.

Tip 2: Tax considerations should be a part of all major financial transactions: buying a house or renting, buying or leasing a car, getting a loan, investing in the stock market. Get professional advice if necessary.

Tip 3: Be realistic in drawing up your budget. Preserve as much as possible the style of life you can afford and want.

Tip 4: If you do use credit cards, the experts suggest you keep your monthly charges and installment payments less than 15 percent of your monthly income.

Tip 5: Save 5 to 10 percent of your income every month. It's important to develop the savings habit as part of your budget.

Tip 6: Keep 10 to 15 percent of your monthly income for recreation, clothing, and home-maintenance costs.

Tip 7: If you want to get assistance from a financial consultant, do all the preliminary work first. Write your questions down before you go.

Tip 8: Both husband and wife should have their own bank accounts in addition to any joint account. The wife's account will help her establish a credit rating if she doesn't already have one.

Tip 9: Budgets, like your body, need ongoing attention. Just as you can't exercise just once and expect to be physically fit, you cannot let your budget remain inactive and expect it to be healthy. Use it and upgrade it when necessary.

Tip 10: Pay off the debt with the highest interest first. This sounds obvious, but a lot of smart people sometimes forget.

Tip 11: Keep your future expenses in mind (a college education, a vacation property) and use your budget to help you meet them.

Tip 12: Teach your children to budget their money. Help them set up and operate a budget. If you teach them healthy attitudes toward money handling and management, they will be less likely to have hangups about money later on.

Chapter 16
Savings and the Unconscious

I once asked a friend what he was saving for. He smiled slyly and replied, "I'm saving for a sunny day." I smiled back and said, "That's an amusing turnabout."

Sound, homey advice on saving prudently goes back at least to Benjamin Franklin. He, unlike my friend, placed a lot of emphasis on saving for a rainy day, and coined the expression, "A penny saved is a penny earned." That saying, like "A penny for your thoughts," was obviously written before modern taxes and inflation came into the picture. Franklin's proverb was altered by Ogden Nash to read: "A penny saved is impossible." Or we could turn to James Reston for his witty analysis: "A dollar saved today is seventy-five cents earned tomorrow."

Any way you look at it, though, the problems surrounding savings are not a laughing matter. There are two primary forms of money-saving headaches: over-saving and under-saving.

In both cases, the person misses the point and gets neurotically caught up in self-defeating behavior. As with all neuroses, these problems with saving money vary in degree and intensity; in their mildest form, they are near to "normal."

In some people, however, these tendencies become *compulsive* (the person feels *compelled* to do things his or her way). If you add to this the *obsessive* element (which makes a person think about something all the time), you have the psychologically more virulent problem of the *obsessive-compulsive* saving personality.

The Compulsive Saver

The compulsive saver neurotically carries thrift to irrational lengths by making it an end in itself rather than a means to an end. This person's extreme behavior is based on her belief that dedicated saving will make her safe and secure. She can, however, change if she alters her beliefs.

This form of money neurosis unfolds from an insecure and anxious childhood. Gerald Tightwad was a prime example. Some compulsive savers have not developed a sense of basic trust. One way they protect themselves from the stress of impending disaster is to focus heavily on the retention of cash revenues.

The Compulsive Under-saver

The less common fiscal malady of under-saving is found in the person who tends to play down the value and importance of money. He therefore saves infrequently and irregularly. Under-savers typically experienced insufficient control during their childhood. There may have also been some discipline problems, which led them to need or expect instant gratification.

As an adult, the under-saver often employs the defense mechanism of denial ("Money is not significant to me. It doesn't matter"). In this way, he obscures some of his real concerns and anxieties about the role of money in his life. Often the defensive mechanism he uses to handle his anxieties is *reaction formation* (attempting to adopt feelings and attitudes opposite to those actually felt and experienced). Under-saving may also be related to the inability to postpone gratification in the interests of long-term planning.

A Case History: Julia

As a saver, Julia took the cake, and she probably would have deposited it in some confectionary bank if she had had the opportunity. She grew up during the Depression and was never fully weaned from its emotional effects. While she did her part to perpetuate her behavior, her mother is definitely entitled to some of the discredit. Julia's mother worked hard and long, though unintentionally, to pass along many of her insecurities to her daughter, who guilelessly absorbed her sense that the world is unpredictable and unsafe.

Julia started by accumulating buttons of all sizes and shapes. (Now, old enough to be a grandmother, she still retains some of her once-prized buttons.) From buttons, she graduated to spools of thread, then to dolls, cereal-box prizes, magazines, and then books and records. And throughout all these ventures she added to her money collection. She started off with foreign and domestic coins in a series of piggy banks. Eventually she went on to open a savings account—a first among her friends.

All around her Julia saw hard times. Her parents were barely managing to get by, and they inadvertently reinforced Julia's anxiety. In her efforts to build herself an emotional shield, Julia turned to avid, almost ritual, savings activities. Any little bit of money she earned or was given was salted away to protect her from the threats she witnessed around her. These early experiences made her feel anxious and insecure, and she unconsciously used money to protect herself.

Julia's preoccupation with saving money interfered with her life (as does all neurotic behavior); she was unable to enjoy her financial resources, and at times this damaged her relationships with others.

Julia was attempting to use her savings to compensate for the inadequacies and anxieties she was experiencing. But no matter how much money she accumulated, it could not fulfill her gnawing, unmet needs.

Before she could profit from therapy, Julia had to feel safe and comfortable in our professional relationship. After building up her trust and confidence, we used Guided Imagery and Letting Go exercises, as well as Role Playing, to assist Julia to free herself. We also used Psychodynamics to interpret her relationships with her parents, and to help Julia understand and facilitate her insights into her behavior.

Julia eventually became much more comfortable with money, and the activity of saving lost some of its emotional ramifications for her. Instead, Julia began to think about saving money as a part of financial planning and management.

A Case History: Sol

Sol, on the other hand, was an under-saver. Sol's parents had been incarcerated in a concentration camp during World War II because they were Jewish. After the war, Sol, his two younger sisters, and his parents emigrated to the United States, where they lived with his uncle's family in New York. With the support of the uncle, Sol's father, who had been a pharmacist before the war, was able to get a job as an assistant in a pharmacy.

Sol's mother and father emphasized the importance of saving as much as possible. Sol responded, in what appeared to be a very robust reversal of his family's priorities, by spending his money without much thought for the next day. It wasn't that he threw it away or handled it irresponsibly. Instead, he rebelled against the constricted atmosphere his parents created around him by denying the need to plan ahead. As Sol grew older, into young adulthood and beyond, his contrariness and neurotic need to do the opposite of what his parents thought he should began to manifest itself in other areas of his behavior.

For example, Sol kept interrupting his career as a successful lawyer (flouting money concerns once again) to do volunteer work around the world, particularly in India. He rationalized his behavior in many ways, failing to see that his disdain for money as well as his unpopular decisions—unpopular with his parents at least—were in fact neurotic ways of trying to break free of his parents' influence. While he verbally ridiculed his parents to others with a kind of bravado that would suggest he was emotionally free from them, quite the opposite was true. He was as neurotically enslaved as ever, but he was enslaved to disobeying rather than to obeying.

Sol was unaware of the hostility that was masked by his offhand attitude toward money—particularly saving some of it. To offset some of the great anger that he felt toward his parents, particularly his father, he unconsciously hurt them in a most sensitive area (money).

It took a long course of psychotherapy to help Sol understand the meaning of his actions and to become aware of the self-destructive elements involved. Much of the work was psychoanalytically oriented therapy, which explored the nature of his early relationships with his mother and father, tracing the role of his unconscious as well as the defense mechanisms in his life.

It took almost a year before Sol was able to sort out his distorted ideas about money and to recognize how self-defeating his attitudes toward saving and valuing money had been. The turning point in his therapy coincided with an experience he had. An opportunity arose for him to buy a superb but costly stereo system. He didn't have the several thousand dollars it required, and even though he could have arranged financing, he was angry at himself for not having sufficient savings set aside. His anger spurred his therapy on. We worked together using the following Green Therapies: Psychodynamics, Cognitive Behavior Therapy, Psychological Flashcards, and Letting Go. Sol's progress, which was slow at first, began to move more quickly as he understood himself better and opened himself more to change.

Why Save?

Have you ever figured out how much money you would have if you had saved a certain sum over a number of years at a given percent of interest? It can be an amusing pastime. For example, one estimate showed that if you saved one dollar a day at 8 percent interest for two hundred years, you (or rather your heirs) would have $4.8 million. That's comforting, isn't it? Then there's the definition I read of a million dollars: the sum that may be honestly acquired by putting aside five hundred dollars every week for forty years!

Our reasons for setting up savings accounts can range from the short-term—a fund for Christmas—to larger, long-term projects, like buying a home. Some people save just to have money set aside for no specific purpose, but surveys indicate that the primary reason for "serious" savings tends to be for old age, when money would be needed in case of illness, disability, or retirement. Money is also tucked away in the event of unemployment or emergencies.

Whatever their goal, most people save for rational reasons. A person who chooses to reduce the potential threats to his well-being by setting aside funds is making a reasonable decision. On the other hand, an individual who constantly attempts to remain one step ahead of her mounting anxiety by frantically saving all the time is acting irrationally. She is not responding to the demands of the real world, but to her own neurotic needs.

Compulsive savers and worriers come in different psychological sizes and shapes. Some go for the small stuff—the pennies. These people are the ones who go to great lengths to save on their utility bills. While it makes good sense to conserve resources and not waste money or utilities, there is a limit. Some people go beyond that limit. When they leave a room, they instinctively shut off all the lights, even if they are returning shortly. And then there are those who go into saving in a big way. They view nickels and dimes as inconsequential as they scrimp on every expense, especially the large ones. They often have lots of money, but drive an old beat-up car.

The Emotional Investment in a Savings Account

Saving money can tap some pretty interesting psychological veins. Many of our hopes, desires, and wishes are tied up with the money we have squirreled away. It can therefore be revealing to explore some of our fantasies about our purposes and plans regarding those funds. Another interesting avenue of exploration concerns our personal history of savings. Try to answer the following questions.

1. Do you have a savings account? If so, what are you saving for?
2. If you could do anything you wanted with the money, what would you do?
3. What memories do you have about saving money when you were a child?

4. What were your family's attitudes toward saving?
5. What attitudes about saving money did you learn from your parents?
6. When you were a teenager, what did you save for—or imagine saving for? Do you still have similar fantasies as an adult?
7. How has the past influenced your present life with regards to savings?
8. Are there any personal changes you would like to make about your personal savings style?
9. Are you prepared to follow the suggested Green Therapies to help you change?

The following table provides a guideline to help you alter problematic attitudes with regards to savings. Explore the table and give the guidelines a chance to be of benefit. Afterward you will be in a more advantageous position to benefit from the next section of the chapter, the How of Savings.

Decide which of the symptoms listed in the left-hand column best describes you. The middle column lists the Green Therapies (Chapters 7 to 14) you might try for the Payoffs described at the right.

Curing Your Savings Headaches

Symptom	Green Therapy	Payoff
If you save in a rigid, inflexible manner and feel the need to save money excessively, try:	Psychodynamics Cognitive Behavior Therapy Thought Stopping Psychological Flashcards	You will gain greater comfort and flexibility in handling your savings.
If you have little overt interest in saving money and tend to spend without planning via savings, try:	Psychodynamics Cognitive Behavior Therapy Psychological Flashcards Letting Go	You will be more aware of the usefulness of saving.
If you are inclined to postpone starting a regular savings program, try:	Assertive Behavior Training Psychodynamics Thought Stopping Psychological Flashcards	You will gain a better understanding of your tendency to procrastinate. You will learn to follow through better with your savings program.
If you save only occasionally and inconsistently, try:	Assertive Behavior Training Cognitive Behavior Therapy Psychological Flashcards Affirmations Guided Imagery	You will improve your planning and organizational skills via increased understanding and practice exercises.

The How of Savings

It would be wonderful if we could take a vitamin-M pill to regulate the absorption and utilization of our money. Alas, no such panacea exists, but a savings program is the next-best thing.

Savings Accounts

Generally speaking, you should have both short-term savings *and* long-term savings and a backup savings account for emergencies or unexpected financial demands.

It's wise to open as many savings accounts as you need to meet your own ends. Check out the different kinds of accounts and the different types of savings institutions: traditional banks, savings-and-loan associations, credit unions, and investment companies. Discuss the matter thoroughly with a well-qualified financial planner or consultant.

Decide which money institution has the best deal for you based on rates of interest, business hours, "grace periods" for withdrawing money and retaining interest, flexible account-closing policies, and minimum balances necessary to earn maximum interest.

A Lifetime Plan

In your twenties or thirties—particularly if you are single—concentrate on being safe and sound. Keep your savings highly liquid (that means you can cash them easily; it doesn't mean you should invest in booze or similar potables). Put your money in an account or investment that is subject to only minor fluctuations and is guaranteed safe.

In order to capitalize on the principle of compound interest, it is essential to start saving early in life. By putting time on your side, you'll soon have your money reproducing itself like our four-legged, white-tailed furry friends.

In your mid and late thirties, your net worth will probably be higher. Benjamin Stein, in his book *Financial Passages*, makes this point clear: "While the average family has only saved about fifteen weeks worth of earnings by the time the head of the household reaches twenty-nine, the average family with a head of household in his or her mid-thirties has been able to save about ten months' income." Liquidity of funds continues to be important through these years, although more adventurous forays into investments can be made, for example, stock purchases, with, of course, help from a professional expert.

Benjamin Stein also reminds us that compound interest is an important part of a saving plan. If you are trying to reach the capital sum of $750,000 when you are sixty-five and if you are able to earn a consistent 11 percent on your money, you would have to save about $5,900 a year starting at age forty. But if you wait until you are forty-five, you will have to set aside about $10,500 a year. The earlier you start saving the better.

In your fifties it is important not to spend your savings. A major monetary question facing a person in his fifties planning for retirement is whether his savings should be arranged so he can live on the interest or whether he should set up an annuity and live on a blend of principal and interest.

Those in their sixties and beyond will find that goods and services continue to cost much the same as they did before retirement. Even though there are important differences between the pre- and post-retirement periods, a good solid savings plan is still important.

Teach Your Children

Saving, and the mentality that goes along with it, should ideally start from day one. Well, maybe not literally from day one. I doubt you want to go so far as to play lullabies with the sound of jingling coins in the background. But as your children grow old enough, teach them to save as part of their money-handling education (see also page 244). The value and benefits of saving should be spelled out and demonstrated and should continue straight on through high school and beyond, when your children may want to save for their education, their career changes, and possibly even marriage.

Psychiatrist James Knight tells us that:

> The child's assessment of reality regarding money can lead to many misinterpretations, often setting the stage for future difficulties in money matters. When a parent sticks to a fixed allowance and refuses to give additional money, a youngster may shout: "You don't love me anymore!" At this point, the child still believes that his parents have an unlimited amount of money which is being withheld from him for parental reasons. Depending on the parents' handling of the situation, the child can make either a good or bad adjustment to the initial shock of not having as much money as he wants. When the child learns his monetary limitations, he must make for himself the choice of whether to save or spend. His management of this crisis will determine much of his attitude about money as an adult.

To prevent the development of psychological money problems, it is important to establish healthy attitudes toward money in children. Love and money should not be confused. Children must learn to make judgments about the way money and affection sometimes get mixed up. ("If you loved me you'd buy me a bicycle." "You love Tommy more than me.") Depending on the circumstances, giving or holding back money can be an act of love. It is important for children to understand that real love cannot be bought for money.

When young children are faced with limitations on the amount of money they can have, or on what they can spend their money on, they may wonder whether to spend the money or save it. They might also have trouble deciding what to buy with it, what to do if they don't have enough to buy what they want, how to ask for more, and what to do if Mommy and Daddy say no. Children can also experience anxiety or anger when they learn that their parents do not have unlimited fiscal resources.

How all these things are dealt with can influence a child's conception of money and determine some of the money patterns he'll have as an adult.

It is useful to have a yardstick against which you can measure the responses of your children. From the age of three years to five years, children tend to believe that money has magical properties; up to the age of five, their emotions about money in general are vague. The years from five to nine are very influential. During that time, a child begins to develop a number of important emotional responses to money—particularly the connection between love and money. From nine to sixteen children develop very clear attitudes to money. Here is a breakdown of the development year by year:

Age	Developmental Money Attitudes
9–10	Most nine-year-olds are very casual about money. They often spend their allowance as soon as they get it. Some save a little, others nothing.
10–11	Children are now more interested in and more careful with money. A few are miserly with their allowance. Some save up for special purchases.
11–12	Some eleven-year-olds save fairly large amounts of money to make important purchases. Some squander their money and tend to be careless with it. Others try to make their money last. A quote from J. Paul Getty (the billionaire) at age eleven: "I now have 275 marbles. Counted my stamps—305."
12–13	Twelve-year-olds tend to be careful with money. A few are still careless, but most are pretty good about saving for presents and large expenditures.
13–14	Individual differences in handling money are quite broad. Some have an exaggerated idea of money, of how much people should earn, and of how much things cost.
14–15	Some supplement their allowances with earnings but they do not have much in the way of savings in the

bank; however, they often have money at home saved for special purchases.

15 and 16   There is almost as much variety among fifteen- and sixteen-year-olds regarding the amount of money available and how it is handled as there is with adults. Part-time and summer jobs are very common. Some try to budget their funds with varying degrees of success. Some save money in the bank. Teenagers generally show a greater appreciation for the value of money.

Here are some points to keep in mind while planning and implementing your savings program:

Tip 1: A family of four should have three to six months of income saved and stashed away for emergencies. Singles, couples, and larger families should decide on the number of months of resource money based on the total capital they would require during a period of duress, such as job loss.

Tip 2: Look for a financial institution that gives you daily compound interest from the day of deposit to the day of withdrawal.

Tip 3: For a true sense of security, turn to money market funds (tried and true) and certificates of deposit.

Tip 4: A savings program works best if you put aside the same percentage of your income each month.

Tip 5: Make certain your savings are fully insured and protected to the maximum coverage. This is particularly true today, when many financial institutions have gotten into serious trouble.

Tip 6: When you think about amassing money through savings, remember that, if you allow twice as many years to accumulate your savings, you only have to put away a quarter as much money to reach your goal.

Tip 7: In general, when you think about savings, consider these factors: your age, your savings goals, the amount you have already saved, the role of inflation, and the best methods for investing your money.

Tip 8: Between the ages of thirty and forty, you should attempt to save (including investments) 5 to 7 percent of your income after taxes. Increase this by 1 to 2 percent until your late forties, after which the goal should be 10 to 15 percent.

Tip 9: When determining your savings plan, remember to be SLY: make sure you include Safety, Liquidity, and Yield.

Tip 10: As with all financial decisions, consider the tax implications. Get expert help if necessary.

Tip 11: Remind yourself that your home and the mortgage on it are part of your savings plan. Paying off a mortgage in excess of the regular payments is a form of savings.

Tip 12: Even if it is still a long way off, think about your retirement and start saving for it (the earlier the better).

Tip 13: Keep in mind that your needs will change over the years—and so should your savings plan.

Tip 14: Remember that a savings program should be realistically built into your overall budget. The amount you save and the reasons you save relate directly to your lifestyle and your philosophy of money.

Tip 15: Help your children develop psychologically healthy attitudes toward savings (and money in general). Use

Savings and The Unconscious

Green Therapies to help yourself first if your mental attitudes are getting in the way.

Tip 16: Realize that to save successfully you have to be able to postpone gratification—sometimes for years. Even if you spend some of your savings for fun (and it's a good idea to have a "fun" account), you still may find it difficult to save regularly. If so, check out your psychological feelings on the subject and use the Green Therapies as needed.

Chapter 17
Paying Your Insurance Dues

Money is best used to pay for goods and services and not to buy emotions (such as love and affection), or states of mind (such as inner peace and contentment). People who try to "cashify" these sentiments always fail. Money cannot fulfill a psychological role or do an emotional job for us. We have to do that for ourselves.

If thinking about life insurance with all its ramifications elicits anxieties and awakens dormant worries, then you need to deal with those psychological issues and get them sorted out. Don't let paying insurance premiums turn into "hush money" to quiet your anxieties. Don't tell yourself that if you buy insurance you won't have to think about your fears of illness and death. On the other hand, don't avoid buying life insurance altogether as a way of quelling your apprehensions about mortality. That doesn't work, either.

In reality we do have to think about the fact that we will die some day, leaving others to survive us. Buying life insurance is a way to gain greater control over the calamitous consequences of unpredictable events. It's a form of psychological protection as well, since it calms our fears about leaving our dependants destitute. And it allows us to hedge our bets by providing a "second-best" alternative in case things turn out badly and we have to accept something less than we might have wished. It is also part of an overall money-management philosophy, which should be solidly based on planning sanely for the future; budgeting, saving, investing, and purchasing life insurance; all the parts of financial management have this quality in common.

Buying Life Insurance

Woody Allen once commented: "After all, you know, there are worse things in life than death. I mean, if you've ever spent an evening with an insurance salesman, you'll know exactly what I mean." His humor covers the discomfort most of us feel when contemplating our own mortality, which is what coming face-to-face with an insurance agent forces us to do.

Those people with money neuroses experience even more anxiety when they discuss life insurance. If Gerald Tightwad were buying life insurance, for example, he would probably tend to be suspicious of the salesperson and of the salesperson's desire to separate him from some of his tightly held dollars. If the agent could see through Gerald she would be able to "score" by playing on Gerald's need to get something concrete and monetary out of everything, even his own death and even if the money went to his heirs.

Sarah Bargainer, on the other hand, might place too much emphasis on the pennies saved on one "fire-sale" insurance policy versus another one. The success of the agent sitting across from Sarah would depend on whether he could make her feel as though she got a "steal."

A Case History: Bob

Let's meet Bob, who can show us how some of these pieces fit together. Bob certainly did not come to me to discuss his feelings about insurance, but that's what we ended up talking about—at least in part.

Bob was forty-seven when he first appeared for counseling. He had been married for five years when he was in his mid-thirties, but he and his wife had split up when his homosexuality became dominant in his life, as it had been years before. Bob hadn't wanted to divorce his wife, whom he still cared for, but he saw divorce as the only response to his growing need to meet men. He was worried about the shortness of his life and felt he needed more time.

Bob originally chose to go into therapy because he had met Theresa, a woman he believed he loved. He wanted to marry her and start a family but he agonized about his own emotional stability in light of his past vacillations. He wanted me to help him work through some of these feelings.

Bob was essentially unsure of himself and often hesitated to act. More often than not, he would allow others to persuade him to their cause. Although he sometimes resented the aggressiveness of others, he tended to repress his feelings because he needed their approval and he believed he got it when he went along with them. He had a hard time saying no.

Bob and Theresa eventually began to live together and later they married. One day Bob came into my office upset about a run-in he had had with a life-insurance agent. Bob was anxious to make financial provisions for Theresa and to put aside some money for the child they hoped to have. The salesperson quickly assessed Bob's overeagerness, his generally passive nature, and his lack of assertiveness, and the agent took advantage of what he viewed as Bob's personal weaknesses. Some insurance agents are taught to assume consent, and that's exactly what this agent was assuming as he pushed Bob gently but firmly to premium costs, which caused Bob to become alarmed.

Bob grew quite angry and restless as this process continued, but he felt impotent to change its course, particularly with Theresa anxiously looking on. In part, his tension was caused by the size of the sums of money involved. He managed to say, almost stuttering, that he would have to think about it. Then he left the room in a hurry, leaving Theresa to look after the agent.

In general, Bob's attitude toward and handling of money was sane, if not always sound. As a tenured teacher he had job security and a pension as well as some group insurance, which came with the job.

Growing up with just his widowed mother to care for him (his father died in a boating accident when Bob was ten) started Bob's fears about financial resources. His father's life-insurance benefits were inadequate to meet his mother's needs and she talked continually about how her husband had let them down financially by not fully providing for their needs.

When Bob was confronted with purchasing a financial safeguard for his family, he retreated psychologically. His memories, combined with his lack of assertiveness, demolished his self-confidence and left him with a general sense of loss of control. The nervousness he experienced with the insurance agent related both to his fears about death and to the past "ghosts" evoked by the memories of his mother's anger and disappointment.

Bob and I first spent time exploring the psychological dynamics of his low self-assertiveness, since it's impossible for a person to change the way he acts without first changing his attitudes. Then we went directly to work on Bob's disquieting symptoms.

The object was to help Bob buy life insurance in an assertive way. The first thing I did with Bob, after establishing his readiness to change, was to take him through several steps with me. He mentally replayed his nonassertive behavior with the insurance agent and wrote down what he thought, felt, and did. We explored the more self-assertive routes he might have taken. He began to formulate tactics he would be willing to try when he invited the salesman back to his home.

We also worked on relaxation techniques, which Bob could combine with the assertiveness training we were doing together. After he spent some time successfully asserting himself in his imagination under relaxed conditions, the moment arrived and Bob confronted the insurance agent, and, using methods we practiced, bought the life-insurance policy he wanted.

Over a period of months—with patience and practice and with reinforcement from me and others—Bob grew to be more personally effective with people and money.

The Fear of Death

Fears about death are universal in our culture. In the past ten or fifteen years, however, the topic has become more open and public with pioneers like Elisabeth Kübler-Ross (author of *Death and Dying*) leading the way. But the taboo still remains.

Our widespread superstitions and fears around this subject lead us to do everything we can to avoid dealing with its terrors. Even the wearing of black at funerals is tied up with the evasion of death. At one time death itself was thought to be a contagious disease, which was passed on by evil spirits who hung around the deceased. If you dressed in black the spirits couldn't see you and therefore you would be free from any potential harm from them.

The desire to hide from death lies deep within us. In a parable called "Death Speaks," author W. Somerset Maugham captures the essence of the futility of such an exercise:

> There was a merchant in Baghdad who sent his servant to market to buy provisions and a little while later the servant came back, white and trembling, and said, Master, just now when I was in the market-place I was jostled by a woman in the crowd and when I turned I saw it was Death that jostled me. She looked at me and made a threatening gesture; now, lend me your horse, and I will ride away from this city and avoid my fate. I will go to Samarra and there Death will not find me. The merchant lent him his horse, and the servant mounted it, and dug his spurs in its flanks and as fast as the horse could gallop he went. Then the merchant went down to the market-place and saw me standing in the crowd and came up to me and said, Why did you make a threatening gesture to my servant when you saw him this morning? That was not a threatening gesture, I said, it was only a start of surprise. I was astonished to see him in Baghdad, for I had an appointment with him tonight in Samarra.

The Insurance Questionnaire

Here are some questions to help you analyze your feelings about insurance:

1. What were your parents' attitudes to life insurance and other forms of insurance (disability, home, car)?
2. When did you first become aware of life insurance? What were your reactions?
3. As an adult, have you had any difficulties in dealing with insurance or with insurance agents?
4. When you think about life insurance, do thoughts of your own death keep you from dealing with it rationally?
5. Have you ever put off buying life insurance? Why?

6. Do you buy the first insurance policy offered or do you check what else is available first?
7. Do you feel that you have all the insurance you (and your family) need?

The Meaning of Insurance

Psychologically speaking, what does it mean for us to insure our lives? What are we symbolically trying to do? We are attempting to avert risk, protect ourselves from uncertainty, and provide a type of guarantee that we will survive in some form or another, even if that form is only money. We are, in fact, dealing with the central existential issue of our lives: our deaths, our mortality.

We tell ourselves we are protecting ourselves from uncertainty and risk by purchasing some peace of mind. We tell ourselves that since we are going to die it is better to provide financially for our loved ones by buying life insurance. Well, yes, it is, but we must not lose sight of the many psychological insecurities and existential doubts we leave unexamined in this process.

We know that purchasing life insurance is not going to enable us to live even one more minute than we would otherwise, but we don't like to think about it. Many of us don't want to focus on these matters, much less do anything about them.

People have a variety of attitudes toward insurance. Some resent having to buy protection; others gain a sense of security from it. When you think of it, what we are doing is putting a price tag on our own lives. The experience of doing so can elicit many different emotions—fear, anger, sadness, and rage—especially among those with the traits associated with neuroses about life insurance. These include: fears about loss of control, anxieties about health and personal well-being, apprehension about mortality and the use of time, and sometimes exaggerated needs for certainty and predictability, which relate to a lack of self-assertiveness.

People who need help in this area include:
- those whose emotions run high when insurance is discussed,

- those who are not decisive and clear about their needs;
- those whose vulnerability tends to be high;
- those who have had past difficulties associated with insurance.

If you have had any difficulties in the past or anticipate any of these problems, turn to the Green Therapies for assistance. After you have fortified yourself, move on to the pragmatic tips and suggestions in the next section of this chapter.

Decide which of the symptoms listed in the left-hand column best describes you. The middle column lists the Green Therapies (Chapters 7 to 14) you might try for the Payoffs described at the right.

Curing Your Life-Insurance Headaches

Symptom	Green Therapy	Payoff
If you worry about death and the idea of buying life insurance or if you are concerned about your personal well-being, try:	Thought Stopping Affirmations Psychological Flashcards Destressing and Systematic Relaxation	You will have control over upsetting thoughts and increased freedom to act. You'll feel more secure about yourself.
If you are distressed by negative beliefs and distorted thinking, or fear you can't handle the responsibility of buying insurance, try:	Cognitive Behavior Therapy Affirmations Psychological Flashcards Assertive Behavior Training Destressing and Systematic Relaxation	You'll increase your ability to challenge your inner messages, and gain greater feelings of self-confidence.

(continued on next page)

Symptom	Green Therapy	Payoff
If you feel overwhelmed and pressured when you face insurance salespeople or are anxious about losing control, try:	Assertive Behavior Training Psychological Flashcards Destressing and Systematic Relaxation Thought Stopping Psychodynamics (Brief) Affirmations	You will bolster your capacity to make independent decisions with greater certainty, and be more assertive handling your money. You will also feel more in control.
If you tend to postpone buying life insurance or put off thinking about money matters, or if you are apprehensive about time, try:	Affirmations Destressing and Systematic Relaxation Assertive Behavior Training Psychological Flashcards	You'll achieve a significant reduction in task avoidance, and be able to plan your time more efficiently with less anxiety.

The How of Life Insurance

The first thing to remember about buying insurance is that insurance salespeople are not impartial. They should not be your first contact for information about obtaining insurance.

Do your homework first. Learn as much as you can from other sources. Then review your life circumstances (age, dependants, direction, goals). Each individual or family has different needs, and the amount of coverage you seek is directly related to an assessment of these factors.

Your Insurance Homework

The main purpose of life insurance is, of course, to replace the income you'll no longer be making after you are dead. Together with other income sources such as investments, employee benefits, pensions, and savings, insurance should theoretically meet the needs of those who survive you.

This fact leaves you with the unhappy and unpopular task of figuring out how much you are worth dead! It's sort of like the posters in the old Western movies—Wanted Dead or Alive!

To figure out the value of your estate (your estate, in this case, means your assets and liabilities, not the four thousand acres of cattle country you one day hope to own), begin by evaluating your current assets:

- the value of your home and other property and real estate you own;
- your investments, including stocks and bonds;
- the value of any pensions or retirement plans;
- all savings accounts;
- money from any and all sources not already included.

Now figure out your liabilities:

- all debts owed;
- taxes due;
- any other possible monies owed.

Subtract the liabilities from the assets. The remainder is the current net worth or value of your estate.

Now, figure out how much income your estate will provide your beneficiaries for how long. In order to decide if that will be enough, look at your monthly budget figures (remember them?). Subtract what it costs to keep you fed, clothed, and housed (sorry, but you won't be needing it). Now, decide how much your dependants would need a month to maintain the lifestyle you would like them to have. Compare these figures with the monthly income from your estate. If these numbers are relatively close together, you don't need life insurance. If not, you do.

How Much You Need

To figure out how much you need, take the additional amount needed and work out how much capital it would take to produce that amount in interest. For example, if your survivors would need $2,000 a month, assuming 6 percent interest, you need $400,000 worth of life insurance.

Kinds of Life Insurance
While there are a multitude of different life-insurance policies available with all kinds of clauses, conditions, and situations, the two major categories are *term life* and *whole life*, which is sometimes called straight life or ordinary life. These names are not based on value judgments (he has an ordinary life; she has a straight life) but on the length of time the policy is in effect.

Term life—similar to fire or automobile insurance—buys you protection for a specified period of time and pays your beneficiary the amount of the policy if you die within that period. The policy and its usefulness end when the period ends.

Whole life, on the other hand, has no time limit. It pays whenever you die.

The kind and the amount of insurance you buy will depend on your age, the amount of coverage you need, the amount you can afford, and the needs of your dependants.

Here are some tips to help you make a wise choice.

Tip 1: Check out the books in your library or bookstore for accurate information to help you understand your insurance choices. Free information is available from the American Council of Life Insurance, the Health Insurance Association of America, and the Canadian Life and Health Insurance Association. Local consumer associations can also be helpful.

Tip 2: Meet with life-insurance agents from at least three different companies or ask a reputable broker who represents at least three companies. Ask questions of each and compare their answers. Consider the clarity of information, the cost of products being sold, and the pros and cons of a variety of policies (term insurance, whole life, and universal life). Take into consideration your feelings about the agent as well. Make notes and request a summary of the highlights of the information supplied. After the meetings, compare the data from all agents.

Tip 3: Include your spouse or dependants in all your insurance planning and decisions.

Tip 4: Ask friends, relatives, and associates about how they handle their insurance needs. Even though everyone's situation is different, it can be helpful to get a variety of opinions. Get recommendations for potential insurance agents from these sources. It can be a good start.

Tip 5: Two basic facts to consider in buying insurance are the number of dependants you have and how long they will need financial help. How much they will need is obviously also very important. Look into these issues carefully.

Tip 6: Be sure to ask your agent how to take inflation into account in insurance calculations. By the time the beneficiary collects (which will, you hope, be a long time from now), inflation may have seriously eroded the value of today's money.

Tip 7: Ask your accountant, lawyer, or financial planner to explain any tax implications associated with your insurance decisions.

Tip 8: In most, if not all, cases, buy term insurance and invest the money you save on the less expensive premiums. Learn for yourself all the pros and cons of term insurance and see what you think. Check it out carefully.

Tip 9: Some experts offer the following rule of thumb to help decide how much insurance you need: if you are a wage earner with dependants and few assets, buy life insurance equal to ten to fifteen times your annual salary.

Tip 10: Remember that life insurance is only one kind of insurance. Other kinds protect you in case of disability, illness or accident, fire, and theft. You can also insure your house or apartment, your car, your office (if self-employed), and your cottage. Review these kinds of insurance with qualified people.

Tip 11: Find out all you can about whatever insurance you may have at your place of employment: group life insurance, medical or dental insurance, and so on. Learn under what conditions you are not covered. Take these policies into account when planning your insurance.

Tip 12: When investigating life-insurance policies, be careful to check out the renewability and medical-examination clauses. In other words, find out what is needed to maintain a policy and to increase it. A renewable policy is preferred.

Tip 13: Before buying, find out exactly how much a policy will cost you in premiums. Also find out about other features, like the conditions under which you can cash in your policy or borrow against it.

Tip 14: Inquire about discounts for special groups: non-smokers, women, homes with special security features (for home insurance).

Tip 15: Set up a fail-safe arrangement for the payments of premiums so there is no chance your policy will lapse.

Tip 16: Put your policies in secure record files with copies of the important details (policy number, type of coverage, amount of premium) in a safety-deposit box. Your spouse (or another relevant person) should have direct access to this information.

Chapter 18
Where There's Not a Will, There's a Nightmare

Writing a will is a psychologically loaded act. For some of us, indicating how our possessions are to be distributed after our death is symbolically equivalent to giving them away. For others, preparing a will is seen as somehow hastening our demise.

Putting It Off Doesn't Help

Since people don't like thinking about their deaths, much less planning for them, it's not surprising that few of us look forward to writing our last wills and testaments. Endless procrastination is the course most of us take—more so than with any other financial matter. Lawyers report that people frequently cancel will-making appointments and, like children delaying their bedtime, find interminable excuses for postponement.

Avoidance and denial are the primary psychological defenses we fall back upon when it comes to our own deaths and the disposal of all that we have acquired in a lifetime. Indeed, most people avoid the writing of a will altogether. That, however, does not stop them from dying or their property from being disposed of. Statistics point out that as many as 70 percent of those who die in the United States and Canada go to their peace without a will—including many lawyers!

I remember vividly discussing with my lawyer the details of my will and my wife's. The predominant feeling was that of unreality. Phrases and sentences like: "Well, if you die before your wife . . ."; "The trust set up for your child . . ."; "You'll need an executor and perhaps an alternate . . ."; whizzed right by my ears and seemed to be addressed to someone else. Making a will is a little like buying life insurance: it's premised on your death.

Coming to terms with your mortality and your attitudes concerning money is what will-writing is all about. The more these issues are worked out in your life the greater the sense of peace and psychological wholeness you stand to gain—and the easier it will be for you to write that will.

A Case History: Nathan

Nathan had not yet come to terms with these matters. A journalist and writer, he was thirty-seven years old and twice divorced, and he thought a great deal about deathlessness. He struggled often with the meaning of life, particularly where he fit into it all, and he had a hard time reconciling the fact that once he was gone that was it—it would be as if he had never been here at all. It troubled him deeply that life was so fleeting and that at best he would survive as a memory. He wanted more but he didn't know how to get it.

Nathan was in the middle of a crisis about meaning in his life in general and about the notion of preparing a will in particular. He had decided that his son from his first marriage would inherit everything he possessed at his death but he had done nothing about it legally.

One of Nathan's outlets—particularly during these hard times—was excessive drinking. He didn't expect alcohol to dispel his sense of purposelessness but he did want to numb his feelings. Nathan was experiencing what meaning therapist Victor Frankl referred to as an "existential vacuum," which evokes the "neurotic triad" of depression, aggression, and addiction. With these furies pursuing him Nathan saw no reason to put together a will; nor did he have the necessary mental stamina to do so.

There were two classic threads involved in Nathan's life: the "normal" realistic concern about the purpose and meaning of life and the neurotic aspects, like his depression and drinking, that often hide covert psychological needs and meanings.

In addition to introducing Nathan to relaxation and stress-reduction techniques, I focused my attention on reviewing with him the philosophy of life that had been guiding him without his awareness. He had developed some of his attitudes when he was younger. Nathan's father had been disabled by a car accident and most of his family's financial resources were spent on his rehabilitation. When his father died a few years later, after a brief stay in the hospital, Nathan was extremely downhearted. Not only did he lose a parent but he also had to give up a favorite fantasy of his: he had hoped that his father would one day open a retail candy and variety store. It never happened.

Nathan's father's will was very easy to probate since after the expenses had been paid there was very little left over from his life-insurance policy. Nathan became quite bitter; he couldn't see the point in anything.

Every time Nathan thought about writing a will his latent anxieties were reawakened. Exploring the issue in therapy was a time-consuming process but Nathan felt better as a result and he slowly assumed a more balanced view of life. His resistance to preparing his will also diminished greatly and he completed the necessary legal papers.

Coming to Terms

If you'd rather have root-canal work done than write your will, consider the following points:
- writing a will is not going to hasten your death;
- if you write your will today, you can forget about it tomorrow;
- estate planning is not just for the rich—if you don't decide who gets what, the government will decide for you and you won't be in a position to complain;
- those who die without a will leave their friends and family in a quandary, and often in a legal mess.

Dying "intestate" (without a legal bequeathal) does not mean what it sounds like—a poor chap who died sometime after having had an orchidotomy (removal of the testes). On some occasions, however, unhappy survivors have been known to think castration a fit and worthy punishment for the deceased who passed on without leaving a will or for leaving one with which they disagreed.

Intimations of Immortality

Since no one has yet figured out a way to buy a way out of death—though we all know it's not for want of trying—people have turned to inheritance as a way of sublimating these urges and purchasing the illusion of immortality. The desire for immortality has been with humankind since its origin. It has manifested itself in vast collections of time-defying jewelry and gold, in gargantuan stone and marble monuments, and in each culture's inheritance customs and laws. One symbol that has come to epitomize immortality in our time is money itself. By passing it on, we allow ourselves to believe, if only for a moment, that our money will live on after us. In order to gain a sense of control over our destinies, we pass on our worldly goods to our descendants through wills and inheritances.

Although it may be only symbolic, your will is a piece of worldly immortality. Think about it.

If those thoughts still make you anxious, consider the following therapeutic guidelines. Decide which of the symptoms listed in the left-hand column best describes you. The middle column lists Green Therapies (chapters 7–14) you might try for the Payoffs at the right.

Curing Your Will-Writing Headaches

Symptoms	Green Therapy	Payoff
If you keep putting off writing a will, even though you know it's important try:	Cognitive Behavior Therapy (Brief) Destressing and Systematic Relaxation Guided Imagery Psychological Flashcards	You'll be able to subdue the doubts that make you procrastinate, and to understand how important writing a will is.

(continued on next page)

Symptoms	Green Therapy	Payoff
If you're unwilling to decide what to do with your money, because you're afraid to think about your own death, try:	Destressing and Systematic Relaxation Guided Imagery Letting Go Psychodynamics (Brief)	You'll feel more comfortable when you think about your own mortality and you'll be able to confront the idea of assigning assets in your will.
If the idea of writing a will overwhelms you because it seems too complicated or if you're anxious about dealing with large sums of money, try:	Destressing and Systematic Relaxation Cognitive Behavior Therapy Psychological Flashcards Guided Imagery Thought Stopping	You'll learn that your thinking about wills is distorted, and you'll be able to view your money and will in perspective.
If you can't decide what to do with your money and feel indecisive about the whole topic, try:	Destressing and Systematic Relaxation Psychodynamics (Brief) Cognitive Behavior Therapy (Brief) Psychological Flashcards Thought Stopping	You'll learn how to work through your feelings of doubt and indecision in setting up the details of your will.

The How of Wills and Estate Planning

One of the most significant components of our financial lives—the planning of our estates—is also the most overlooked. After all, who wants to talk about death—especially our own. But estate planning, despite its terminology, should really be seen for what it is: a rational and organized method of passing on your total worldly possessions to your heirs and beneficiaries.

What Your Will Does

Your will—the main tool of estate planning—offers you a degree of immortality by giving you control over your monetary affairs after your death. Estate planning basically involves the development of a program to insure that your wishes are implemented and that your possessions and the people you care about are taken care of after you are gone.

Our legal system grants us an extremely important right (which, needless to say, was not always given to all members of society): the right to determine what happens to our accumulated wealth when we die. And even though our wishes may be limited in certain respects by laws or by a judge's discretion, we can, by and large, make whatever requests we want. It would be incredibly foolish not to take advantage of this right, and yet a large number of people fail to leave a will.

The object of estate planning is, of course, to make sure that what you leave behind gets to the people you designate at the right time and at the least possible cost to the estate. To do this, you may need the help of professionals: a lawyer, financial experts, and an accountant. Choose professional advisors who are experienced in the field. Interview several people to make sure you get the best one for the job.

Help Writing Your Will

Your will should ideally be written by an experienced lawyer so that it conforms to all legal requirements. In that way, when the will is probated, there should be no problems in establishing its validity. When other types of wills are prepared—such as a *holographic will* (written by the testator in his own handwriting) or a *nuncupative will* (spoken by a dying person)—substantial legal problems could arise in sorting out the estate.

Trusts

In the event of your death, it may be advisable to set up trusts—for children, spouses, or others. (Trusts are ways of deferring the receipt of income and capital.) You need the advice of your lawyer and a trust consultant in this matter. If the trust is to run for a long time, you may want to have it administered by a trust company rather than an individual. Once again, expert input is essential.

Set out the conditions under which your executor or trustee can act on behalf of the estate (for example, to maximize investments or related affairs), but be sure that your will is written in a flexible manner. Don't unduly restrict your executor's decision-making powers, particularly when it comes to financial conditions that alter over time.

Here are some tips to help you approach will-writing more willingly:

Tip 1: If you want to have your estate wishes honored, carried out, and protected, you must prepare a bona fide last will and testament that fully conforms to all of the legal requirements of your place of residence. If you leave no will, the laws of the land will take over control according to the government's dictates.

Tip 2: Do everything you can to educate yourself on how to prepare an estate plan. Read books and other resource material on putting together a will and on other aspects of estate planning. After you have done all your preparation, visit an expert. Don't try to save money in this matter. Get the best help available.

Tip 3: Your estate planning could require expert advice from your lawyer, an accountant, an insurance broker and a personal financial advisor. The actual work should involve your spouse in all aspects.

Tip 4: As with all financial-management goals, you should also start your estate planning at the beginning by drawing up a statement of assets and liabilities, reviewing your long- and short-term budget requirements, and writing down your objectives regarding your estate.

Tip 5: Draw up an estimate of the approximate income your family would require in the event of your death. The figures you use should be realistically geared to maintaining the standard of living you would like for them, allowing for inflation.

Tip 6: Remember that you and your spouse should both draw up wills and do your estate planning together. Be sure to make provisions for your children in the unlikely event that the two of you die at the same time. Appoint a guardian to care for your children under such circumstances and make sure financial arrangements are made for the children's futures.

Tip 7: Learn some of the terminology of estate planning. The person who makes out a will is a *testator* (male) or *testatrix* (female) and the person or institution who handles the affairs of the estate is called the *executor* (male) or *executrix* (female). In the unlikely event that you die without a will—*intestate*—the court will appoint an *administrator* (male) or *administratix* (female). The court proceeding in which the validity of a will is established is called a *probate*. The person who died is the *decedent*; a *beneficiary* is a person who receives an inheritance, and the *bequest* or *legacy* is the specific property or money he or she receives. In a *universal legacy* everything goes to one person; divided in fractions it's a *general legacy*; and a specific sum of money or asset set aside for certain people listed in the will is called a *particular legacy*.

Tip 8: One of the most critical factors in estate planning is selecting an executor (or executors). This choice must be made very carefully since the person (or persons) will be handling all the details of your will, including distributing your assets, money, and possessions according to your instructions, as well as disposing of your debts and any other related matters. Discuss the matter with the prospective executrix, giving her a list of the duties she will be called upon to perform. Remind her that estate administration is time-consuming and psychologically demanding. Hiring someone to be an executor can cost 2 to 5 percent of the estate—an expensive alternative.

Tip 9: Make yourself familiar with the demands of an executor. The executor should be aware that he will need the assistance of a lawyer in administering the estate. A partial list of the executor's duties includes: making funeral arrangements; finding the will and reading it; having the lawyer probate the will and obtaining from the court letters of testamentary that formally give him authority as an executor (if he is not a family member); becoming aware of the immediate financial needs of the family; notifying all the beneficiaries, compiling a list of all assets and their value and liabilities and their dollar figures; paying all debts and expenses; disposing of all claims; and then distributing what is left to the heirs.

Tip 10: Although it may seem obvious, be aware that it's necessary to have your will vouched for by a witness. What is not obvious is that if a beneficiary serves as a witness she could lose her legacy even though the will may be legal.

Tip 11: Once the will is completed, sign one copy and leave it with your lawyer. Keep copies in your financial record folders at home. Inform your spouse and executor of the whereabouts of your will.

Tip 12: If you move, remarry, divorce, separate, or undergo any major change in your life, check out the possible implications for your will and estate.

Tip 13: Remember, the will you write may save the financial lives of those you love. Don't put off preparing one, no matter what your age or the size of your estate.

Tip 14: Keep in mind that while taxes are not everything, they form a vitally important part of any estate planning. In order to minimize the taxes on your estate, obtain the counsel of an expert in the field.

Tip 15: Do not leave major nontechnical decisions about the disbursement of your estate to your advisors. The decisions about who gets what and how much should be decided by you and your spouse.

Tip 16: Don't forget that in many situations only your legal spouse will be recognized by law. If you are living with someone to whom you are not legally married, talk to a lawyer about that person's inheritance rights.

Tip 17: Review the details of your will and total estate plan at least once every two or three years. Review them also if you relocate to a place with different inheritance laws, make a significant change in your financial picture, get married, get divorced, separate, have children, or if there are changes in tax laws or if the executor or trustee named in the will dies.

Chapter 19
Taxes: Peace of Mind Despite the Inevitable

Taxes are such an emotional issue that I can imagine someone someday pleading temporary insanity in a tax-evasion case.

Tax time especially is a crazy time. Citizens in substantial numbers throughout the land break into a sweat, hives, or a panic as they watch the grim-reaper taxman swing his scythe through their accumulated dollars. This is prime time for irrational money behavior and depression. Tax lawyers, accountants, and financial advisors confirm what the statistics indicate: there is an increase at tax-time in destructive acts like suicide threats and family-abuse cases, and in anti-social behavior such as bank robberies and burglaries. One woman was so overwhelmed with tax anxiety that she threatened to end it all by killing herself.

Taxing Problems

Neurotic attitudes about money frequently play a role in our resistance toward paying taxes. Here are some of the psychological responses I have come across. See if you share any of these views on taxes:
- "I feel exploited and ripped off."
- "I feel victimized. I'm paying more than my fair share."
- "Sometimes I want to get even."
- "Others are getting away with paying less than they should. Why can't I?"
- "I don't believe I'm getting that many benefits in return for my taxes."
- "It isn't all that serious to hold back some of my money."
- "I need the money much more than the government does."
- "People with a lot of money can pay someone to significantly

reduce their taxes. I'm angry that I can't afford the high-priced help."

Reluctance to part with your dollars for tax purposes obviously doesn't automatically make you a money neurotic. But recall Richard Tycoon. His obsession with amassing wealth interfered with a dispassionate handling of his taxes. He had learned from his father that a penny kept from the taxman was two pennies saved. From those relatively few hours spent with his father during his teens, he remembered hearing something about "before-tax and after-tax" dollars. He gleaned from these meetings that somehow this was a critical distinction to be kept in mind as he built up his financial resources. As an adult, Richard's neurotic money drive, including his obsession with reducing taxes, interfered with the quality of his life.

Sarah Bargainer pacified her anxieties by trying to buy things for less money, by accumulating petty savings, by outsmarting the seller, and by knowing others were paying more. Her attitudes toward taxes fit in with her early feelings of being exploited. She tended to argue with the income-tax department over minor matters, much as she haggled with salespeople, to get special treatment. In general, though, she felt taxes were an area in which she couldn't bargain, and that upset her.

People who are neurotic about their taxes tend to exhibit "cluster traits," such as an impeded ability to give and share; strong competitive feelings, which have crowded out a sense of cooperation; problems with trust, fairness, and justice; and an inclination toward suspiciousness.

A Case History: Ned

Ned had many of these personality features working against him. He did not rush into my office to tell me he had a phobia about taxes. In fact, this forty-six-year-old policeman came to me because he had been suffering from depression.

Ned was married with three children and he pursued at least a half-dozen active hobbies. Unlike the stereotype of the policeman, Ned was artistic in temperament. He liked to paint, take photographs, and tend the flowers in his garden. He was also an inveterate collector, filling his garage, basement, and attic with a lifetime's worth of magazines, books, photographs, slides, and other assorted goodies. Ned took his collections and interests quite seriously and constantly vied with others for superior standing.

Ned never gave much thought to planning his finances, and he was therefore quite relieved that a number of money decisions, such as taxes, group life insurance, and pension plans were made by his employer and the government. His only concern took the form of resentment about the drain on his funds. But on a day-to-day basis, he could compete with Sarah Bargainer as to who could apply the tighter grip on the dollar.

As the years passed, Ned began to think more and more about his retirement. Even though he had a reasonable pension he wanted to improve his monetary position. He got some financial advice and he started to put money into mutual funds and stocks and bonds. This began a few years before he came to see me.

His investments did well, and he became subject to extra taxation on the money he was making. He resented paying additional taxes. He didn't think they were fair or just, and he had a hard time giving up the money.

Things began to get out of hand when Ned grew taciturn and surly. His wife urged him to seek counseling and he came to me shortly thereafter.

It turned out that Ned was going through a lot of inner turmoil. He was suffering from guilt feelings, anger, and doubts. He knew he had to pay his share of income tax on his additional earnings, but he was fighting with himself over doing so. He even began to think of ways to evade paying his taxes. When we explored it together it became apparent that the money was, once again, a symbol of deeper concerns.

As a child, Ned had been blamed for fights and conflicts that arose with his younger brother and sister. In many instances, he was not at fault and he felt victimized. Ned attempted to combat his sense of victimization by compulsively holding on to the only substantial security blanket he had—his financial resources.

To help Ned deal more effectively with the cluster-trait money problems (issues of trust, sharing, fairness, and suspiciousness), we did the Money Psychohistory exercises (see pages 76-77). Then I asked Ned some questions about money.

NF: When you were a child, what were you told about money?

Ned: Money wasn't talked about much in my family, or at least not in front of me and my brother. I really learned about it only later on, particularly in junior high school and high school, when I worked at odd jobs to supplement my allowance. I was always running around trying to get jobs before the other kids got them first. I learned that money was something you get and keep—and occasionally spend—and don't talk about very much.

NF: What views did your mother and father have toward money? How did these views affect you?

Ned: My parents—particularly my father—tended to use money as a power tool to get us to do what they wanted. In order for us to be rewarded, we pretty well had to conform to their wishes. I think these attitudes made me feel insecure and angry at times. I didn't like the feeling of dependency.

NF: How did your attitudes about money change as you grew up?

Ned: Unfortunately, I think I modeled myself on my father in certain ways. Even though I didn't think much about money—in the sense of being preoccupied about it—I tried to acquire as much as I could by saving because I didn't want to be in the position of asking for it.

NF: What are your reasons for wanting to have money? Have your attitudes changed?

Ned: Money for me is a way of protecting myself from possible hurts in the world. It gives me a sense of security and I don't find it all that easy to share it. I think I've had these feelings for a long time.

NF: Has acquiring money in the past satisfied your reasons for wanting it?
Ned: Basically it has. The problems come in when I have to give it out.

The Green Therapies we used together were Destressing and Systematic Relaxation, Guided Imagery, and some Cognitive Behavior Therapy principles.

Avoiding and Evading Taxes

Ned's reluctance to pay some of his taxes was part of a larger societal picture with a long and, according to some, dishonorable history. In 1789, Benjamin Franklin said, "In this world nothing is certain but death and taxes." But many people choose to diminish the tax certainty as much as possible. Though a number of us accept the inevitable with emotional equanimity, others enter into a wide spectrum of rebelliousness, some of it more neurotic than the rest.

The major channel in this direction (and one that is not necessarily neurotic) is the "underground economy." "Working off the books" is just one of the expressions used to describe this threat to the modern tax system: the practice of not reporting taxable income. Most of our financial transactions are recorded and taxed, but if goods and services are paid for in cash (with no record kept) or if goods and services are exchanged in a cashless transaction (bartering), the government may never learn about them. These transactions have led to astronomical losses to government treasuries. Estimates for the United States, for example, range up to almost $100 billion in unpaid taxes, and as high as $315 billion in unreported earnings.

This major economic problem is found in other countries besides the United States, including Canada, Italy (where it's called the "underwater economy"), France, Germany ("black work"), and England ("fiddling"); and it's a major threat to these economies because it distorts the whole system of budgets, allocations, and financial statistical predictions. It also undermines the morale of the taxpayers who are not part of the underground economy.

In 1979, the United States Internal Revenue Service commissioned a survey on tax morality. It was conducted by a private research firm and was based on interviews with almost five thousand people in fifty different communities. The findings were that: "Americans are cheating more (and enjoying it more) and feel less guilty about it perhaps than ever before. One person in five admitted to understating income, one in ten overstated deductions and one in six claimed dependants illegally. More than half said they thought nearly everyone would cheat if he could get away with it." Indications are that these trends are still going strong in the eighties.

Some people rationalize their resistance toward paying money out for taxes by saying that cheating the government isn't a particularly serious crime. To make tax evasion personally more acceptable, and thus reduce the internal anxieties they experience, some people say that tax evasion is just slightly more serious than stealing a bicycle! Such thinking makes us wonder if these people are evading or hiding other things.

Paying Your Dues

If you have experienced undue stress and anxiety in dealing with taxes, it may be part of a larger money neurosis—a distorted attitude you have built up over the years. To determine if this is the case—or if it is a minor monetary headache instead—you should begin by reviewing your thoughts and feelings concerning income taxes. Start by answering the Money Psychohistory questions (pages 76-77) and by closely and honestly reviewing what you do and think about your fiscal affairs with particular reference to taxes.

After this self-examination, refer to the chart to help decide which Green Therapies would help you feel more at ease with yourself. Once you settle these issues, turn to the next section, which contains practical information on taxes.

Decide which of the symptoms listed in the left-hand column best describes you. The middle column lists the Green Therapies (Chapters 7 to 14) you might try for the Payoffs described at the right.

Curing Your Tax Headaches

Symptom	Green Therapy	Payoff
If you think you're being taken advantage of—paying more money in taxes than others—try:	Destressing and Systematic Relaxation Thought Stopping Psychological Flashcards Cognitive Behavior Therapy	You'll be able to distinguish neurotic reactions from legitimate grievances.
If you get apprehensive about filling in your personal income tax form and tend to do it late, and with resistance, or if you have a hard time parting with money, try:	Psychodynamics Cognitive Behavior Therapy Destressing and Systematic Relaxation Affirmations Psychological Flashcards	You will feel more at peace with the demands you face, and better able to eliminate counterproductive thinking.
If you are just generally anxious about taxes and personal finances, try:	Destressing and Systematic Relaxation Psychodynamics Cognitive Behavior Therapy Thought Stopping Psychological Flashcards	You'll gradually increase your ability to handle money and tax affairs without worrying.
If you're compulsive and exaggeratedly concerned with including every last cent when you prepare your tax return, try:	Destressing and Systematic Relaxation Psychodynamics Cognitive Behavior Therapy Affirmations Thought Stopping	You'll feel more free to act responsibly and accurately, without feeling driven about money matters.

The How of Taxes

Even though we do not have to know all the tax rules and regulations, we most certainly need to approach the subject in a mature and adult fashion. We do not have to be experts, we just have to be knowledgeable. A professor of accounting told me that he just follows the directions contained in his tax-return booklet. That is all he needs.

The basis for solid tax planning is the maintenance of thorough records, scrupulous attention to the documentation of your expenditures and related matters, and a complete awareness of the deductions to which you are entitled.

In general, your tax strategy should be aimed at using every legal means to reduce your income-tax obligations. For example, it usually makes sense to arrange your affairs so that taxable income from financial transactions will be submitted for assessment during a year when your taxable income is lower.

Even if you use a professional tax service, it is a good idea to go through your own tax form step by step. It will help you see your taxes in perspective and will aid you in your overall financial planning. If you find that you are caught up in delays or procrastination, refer to the Green Therapies for assistance.

Here are some more tips to help you:

Tip 1: Take the time to inform yourself about the tax strategies you need. Begin by reading popular books and magazines on taxes and tax planning.

Tip 2: The only way tax advantages can be maximized is through year-round tax planning. This must be an ongoing process rather than one that happens only the night before the deadline. However, if you are a full-time employee and your taxes are deducted by your employer, your tax-planning strategies will be more limited than if you are a self-employed or in another special situation.

Tip 3: One of the most critical elements in financial planning is to think of your income in terms of after-tax dollars.

Your disposable income is the cash left over after your taxes have been paid.

Tip 4: Investigate the area of tax shelters if you think you might be interested. Get professional advice about the tax implications and the soundness of the shelter.

Tip 5: Many people pay more taxes than necessary, or fail to take the deductions to which they are entitled. Get the expert help you require to prevent this from occurring.

Tip 6: Many financial decisions affect your taxes. Consult your accountant or financial planner about the tax implications of such things as borrowing money for investments, using your home for business purposes, purchasing a second home, and so on.

Tip 7: Try to arrange your financial activities—for example, borrowing money or investing funds—so you can deduct the interest you pay or receive.

Tip 8: If you are married, plan your tax strategies together. Find out what tax benefits your marital status gives you.

Tip 9: Make a list of the deductions to which you are entitled. Be completely familiar with the expenses you can write off.

Tip 10: With professional assistance, thoroughly explore any tax shelters or tax deferral programs like retirement savings plans.

Tip 11: Check out what money and assets you can pass along to your children for tax-deduction purposes. Explore the possibilities of "income splitting" with your tax advisor.

Tip 12: Tax credits reduce tax obligations. Find out how they work and which ones you're entitled to.

Tip 13: Prepare your tax forms as early as possible, then review the basics: the listings of your income, the expenses, legitimate deductions, and the exemptions to which you are entitled. Double check all your arithmetic calculations.

Tip 14: Choose your tax preparer and expert carefully. Get good referrals, compare costs, and go to a reputable firm.

Chapter 20
Taking Stock of Yourself and Your Investments

The marketplace, whatever its size and location, is a major battleground for money neurotics. Our feelings, including greed, fear and envy, play a significant role in the internal skirmishes that lead to financial decisions. Decisions about investments are particularly fraught with conflicts caused by our emotional immaturity and our uncertainty about our priorities.

Our monetary choices are often guided by an "invisible hand." For example, a neurotic need for power (the invisible hand) may cause us to make financial decisions that are otherwise not in our best interests. If we don't know what money means to us, we are likely to continue behaving neurotically, and the invisible hand will remain in control. If we invest money with the intention of meeting emotional needs, then those needs will continue to go unmet.

The pitfalls of faulty money behavior are endless. One favorite neurotic trick many misguided souls perform is to personalize their investments; they give the stocks and bonds they select a heart and mind of their own. These people, who apparently need to feel very special, initiate a kind of unilateral love affair with their common-stock certificates and feel hurt, annoyed, or even jilted if the paper value fades. They endow the stock market with magical properties, like the mirror in the story of Snow White, and they use it to convince themselves that they (or their stocks) are the fairest in the land.

Likely Candidates

You are likely to act neurotically where your investments are concerned if you have the following "cluster traits":

- a tendency to personify investments and thereby unconsciously endow them with human emotions;
- a strong need to seek approval;
- an inclination to think of yourself as special and favored (common among only children and children who were constantly in the family spotlight);
- a tendency to worry frequently about things going wrong;
- a compulsive absorption with the pros and cons of risk-taking behavior;
- a tendency to project your hopes, wishes, and dreams onto the pot of gold at the end of the rainbow;
- problems controlling your impulses.

A Case History: Geraldine

For many people who get caught up in the stock market—and, indeed, in investments in general—conflict is a way of life. Geraldine was such a person.

Geraldine's father was a Dr. Jekyll and Mr. Hyde type. Half the time he was debt-ridden and the other half he was intoxicated. When he drank, his more destructive and mean sides surfaced and he was quite intolerable. When he was sober he tried to make a go of his small variety store, but with little success. He frequently was away from home, so Geraldine didn't know him very well.

Geraldine's mother, on the other hand, was an overorganized, compulsive woman with a lot of hostility toward her profligate husband. During Geraldine's early years there was a great deal of conflict and tension in the home.

This atmosphere tended to make Geraldine quite insecure. She withdrew in fear and—although she was not aware of it—anger at her father's insensitive behavior. Geraldine sometimes felt deficient and tried to compensate for her imagined shortcomings. She became a rather hesitant and withdrawn teenager, feeling very much an outsider. These traits pursued her relentlessly into adulthood, modified and refined somewhat by experience.

Despite her father's poor money dealings, he had managed to

leave her some money in his will when he died. Geraldine's mood swings, distantly related to the splits in her father's behavior, made her alternate between almost manic highs, where she would invest money in stocks and bonds with wild abandon, and quiet, inverted periods when she worried about the few investments she did make. This business with her father's money was getting Geraldine down. She, like her father before her, worried constantly about things going wrong.

When Geraldine came to see me, she was a lab technician, married for the second time with three children and a husband who loved her but grew more exasperated with her by the hour. He believed that her tendency to be distrustful, controlling, and somewhat antisocial was interfering with their lives. He felt her problems were traceable to her family roots.

We approached Geraldine's conflicts both behaviorally and analytically. Part of the psychological mystery of Geraldine's erratic behavior had to do with the symbolic and unconscious meaning she had given to the money she inherited from her father. At times she ascribed almost an evil quality to the inheritance. At these moments she thought of it as the classical "filthy lucre," and she strove wildly to get rid of it, although she could not consciously throw it away. When these feelings took a holiday, she would replace the guilt she felt at having the funds with fantasies of her lost father and the love she had longed for from him. When she began to recognize the reasons behind her actions, Geraldine was on her way to understanding some of her unsound behavior.

To assist Geraldine in the ever-seductive yet highly elusive process of change, I introduced her to Destressing and Systematic Relaxation. This technique helped relieve some of her stress. I also reviewed some of the techniques of Letting Go and Psychological Flashcards.

The object was for Geraldine to gain a better conviction, composure, and self-assurance in her personal financial explorations and discoveries. She achieved this and improved her personal identity in the process.

Fiscal Identity

Geraldine's inability to handle her investment money effectively related directly to her lack of insight into herself. The danger for all investors in the stock market, or other fiscal venues, is that if they haven't worked out their financial identities before getting involved, they will probably become even more lost afterward. If they use money symbolically to meet certain needs then the satisfactions gained will also be symbolic, the real needs will remain unfulfilled, and the process will go on.

The wish, for example, to seek others' approval through monetary coups, to show superior dollar prowess and acumen among peers, or to gain status and entry into the rarefied strata of wealthy society may drive certain people to the limits of neurotic behavior.

Much of this kind of behavior relates to the fact that, in our culture, money-making is a way of keeping score with our neighbors. Most of us carry scorecards with us wherever we go. If you think back in your life, you are bound to come up with memories in which you compared yourself with others on the money scale. Recalling these times will teach you a lot about the origins of your money attitudes.

A Case History: Ted

Ted's parents provided virtually no practical money education. They did, however, pass on their attitude toward finances, which was negatively colored by his mother's constant harping about dollar expenditures. She was obsessed by money but she never enjoyed any of it. From her Ted acquired an aversion to greenbacks, which he was totally unaware of for many years. In fact, his interest in books, literature, and the arts contributed to his negative money views and led him to believe that money was a necessary evil—but an evil nevertheless.

Perhaps his avoidance of banknotes had to do with his idealization of life and a growing conviction of the incompatibility between life values and financial values. Ted's perception of money had gone to an extreme opposite to that of the person possessed by the proliferation of investments and their payoffs.

Ted came to see me in his late twenties because he found himself unhappy, rather repressed in his social relations (he didn't go out with women very often), and generally lost. Having denied the importance of money in his life, he left himself with just enough to get by. His thoughts would never have turned to investments except in negative terms.

As we worked together, Ted came to realize that he had an exaggerated need to debunk what he took to be the common view of the usefulness and value of money in people's lives. He had believed that being what he called a "capitalist" was, in effect, being a traitor to the values and beliefs of his associates and friends; therefore he would not allow himself to use money as a means of making additional money. Instead he favored a more peaceful and non-competitive view of life.

As we explored the underlying psychological landscape, it became clear that thoughts about finances—especially about investments and fiscal growth—were, in fact, threatening Ted, who felt such thoughts would cause him to lose some of his identity and to become disloyal to the non-material part of himself. He also worried about failure, about taking chances, and he worried—as did his mother—about the consequences of not having enough money.

Ted, like Jerry Rubin, the former radical activist who reportedly was last seen in a suit and tie working on Wall Street, went through different personal stages. He came to understand that he did not have to become an entrepreneur or a big stock wheeler-dealer, to pay some realistic attention to the role of financial investments in his life. He also became aware that many of his views could exist side by side with his revised fiscal insights without creating inner disparities. Money and his politics could mix. Ted looked into something called "ethical investing," which helps people to invest their money in undertakings that are compatible with their conscience, their values, and their beliefs.

It took three or four months before Ted was able to benefit from the Green Therapies we worked on: Destressing and Systematic Relaxation, Cognitive Behavior Therapy, Psychological Flashcards, and Thought Stopping. The breakthrough came when he was able to learn that a healthy interest in money and his personal ideology need not be in conflict.

Playing the Market

Our emotions play a significant role in determining if we invest, how we invest, and when we invest our money. This was true with Geraldine and Ted as well as with the "money-type" people—Gerald Tightwad, Joyce Spendthrift, Richard Tycoon, Sarah Bargainer, and Larry Gamble. People look to the stock market and similar financial vehicles for a solution to their unfulfilled wishes. Each sees something different in it. They try to find in its basically unstructured configurations an answer to their needs and they see in the rise and fall of the ticker-tape elegant and meaningful images.

Yet despite the intricate morass of sophisticated formulas, charts, and computer printouts, there are those who believe that stock prices cannot be accurately predicted. Many have attempted to harness the "green giant," and many have failed. It has been said that we would do just as well if we let a blindfolded monkey throw darts at the stock listings. Srully Blotnick, in his book on investing, tells us that he followed the machinations of 1,103 investors for ten years, from 1966 to 1976, to determine who succeeded in the market and who failed. He discovered that: "The largest losses were suffered by the most knowledgeable and sophisticated players. No one who desperately wanted to make a fortune made one. Only 53 of 1,103 made sizeable gains and a mere handful, four of the fifty-three, did exceptionally well." It doesn't exactly make you want to call up your broker!

How do we get into these messes? John Spooner, author of *Confessions of a Stockbroker*, informs us that his "merchandise" is easy to sell because what he's really selling are dreams of glory—and they always sell themselves. And what's more, he tells us, the occupation of stockbroking will always be around "as long as there is a psychic and emotional need for the kind of therapy we perform."

Mr. Spooner's brave words notwithstanding, there are some serious occupational hazards associated with his kind of work. Stock insanity is more common than even Spooner might have speculated. Money disorders can sometimes take rather bizarre turns as, for example, in the case of the Pittsburgh physician, Dr. Grover Phillippi. According to the Associated Press wire service:

> Dr. Phillippi pleaded guilty to kidnaping and conspiracy for dressing up like Santa Claus and abducting his stockbroker, Robert Haye, from a Christmas party in December, 1983. He lured Mr. Haye into a van and drove into a remote area in West Virginia, where he held him hostage for 11 days, trying to make him confess to mishandling his [Dr. P's] stocks.

The point is that people can go off the monetary deep end when they lose sight of the healthy role of money in their lives.

If you haven't been able to sort these matters out to your satisfaction, they are probably getting in the way of maximizing your investment instincts. Refer to the Green Therapies—particularly Destressing and Systematic Relaxation, Guided Imagery, Psychological Flashcards, Cognitive Behavior Therapy, and Letting Go.

Decide which of the symptoms listed in the left-hand column best describes you. The middle column lists the Green Therapies (Chapters 7 to 14) you might try for the Payoffs described at the right.

Curing Your Investment Headaches

Symptom	Green Therapy	Payoff
If you have a neurotic need to invest money—and sometimes feel uneasy or anxious when you're not investing, try:	Psychodynamics Cognitive Behavior Therapy Affirmations Letting Go Psychological Flashcards Destressing and Systematic Relaxation	You will have a better idea about your purposes and goals in money investing, and you'll be able to make decisions from a more realistic base.
If you fear the risk involved in financial investments or worry about money because you are insecure or overcautious, try:	Psychodynamics Cognitive Behavior Therapy Psychological Flashcards Destressing and Systematic Relaxation	You will be able to more realistically appraise the risks of investing, and will not attach so much emotion to objective financial facts.
If you tend to be impulsive about handling investments or if you have unrealistic expectations concerning the returns you will get, try:	Destressing and Systematic Relaxation Cognitive Behavior Therapy Psychodynamics Psychological Flashcards Thought Stopping	You'll increase your control of your investing, and will be more able to judge financial risks.

(continued on next page)

Symptom	Green Therapy	Payoff
If you invest beyond your means or overspend at the market, and if you tend to gamble when you make investments, try:	Cognitive Behavior Therapy Psychodynamics Psychological Flashcards Thought Stopping	You'll be able to see the self-destructive elements in your own behavior, and this will lead to far more balanced money decisons.
If you are too rigid or too flexible about money, if you can't let yourself go or have a hard time making choices and decisions about investments, try:	Psychodynamics Cognitive Behavior Therapy Destressing and Systematic Relaxation Psychological Flashcards Thought Stopping Affirmations Guided Imagery	It will be easier for you to be more elastic, so you'll be better able to manage your finances.
If you have trouble admitting mistakes and losses, or problems dealing with disappointment and reversals, try:	Cognitive Behavior Therapy Psychodynamics Destressing and Systematic Relaxation Letting Go Affirmations Guided Imagery	You'll come to terms with not being perfect, and you'll begin to accept your personal limitations.

(continued on next page)

Taking Stock of Yourself and Your Investments

Symptom	Green Therapy	Payoff
If you get depressed when you do very well with investments, or if you tend to overwork or have family problems after a financial coup, try:	Psychodynamics Cognitive Behavior Therapy Destressing and Systematic Relaxation Guided Imagery Psychological Flashcards Thought Stopping Affirmations	You may come to terms with your own needs, and begin to understand your pursuit of money and your response to it.

The How of Investing

It's fascinating how an insight into one segment of our lives can enlighten us about other parts of our lives. For example, helping parents and their children with school problems, I began to wonder how many parents know what is expected of their children at school. After all, how could they evaluate and maximize their child's progress if they didn't have the larger picture firmly in mind?

Investments are like that, too. As part of your investment plan, you should ask three questions:
- What financial practices have I used up to this point?
- How successful was I?
- What do the money specialists and resource materials have to offer?

It is always important to know what came before in order to make the most of what comes afterward.

Getting Ready

Start out by reviewing where you are at this time. Gather together all the relevant information: a recent budget, your net-worth statement, your last year's tax form, and your investment records. Examine the investments you have made up to this point. Look for errors you think you have committed, and what steps you have taken to work more effectively with your funds.

As part of this process you might want to get some professionals on your team—a lawyer, an accountant, a financial planner, a stockbroker. If you don't have a team, select people with whom you feel at ease, whom you trust, and whom you know are highly qualified.

Review your ideas with these people and read books and magazines on the subject. Then, combining the best thoughts you have gleaned from all sources, formulate your overall investment plan.

A sane approach to setting investment goals must include a consideration of two primary factors: a financial personality picture and a financial life plan. The clearer you are about the psychological meaning money has in your life, the greater your chances of maximizing its use.

Your Financial Personality

Your personal attitudes and feelings are directly related to your financial goals, and they determine the kind of investments you should make. In other words, there should be a good fit between your personality and the type of investments you choose. One important factor would be how comfortable you feel with different degrees of risk. If you are not much of a risk taker, then the commodities market or buying stocks on margin wouldn't be for you. A related factor is your ability to sustain loss. For example, would you sell a stock in order to cut your losses?

Remember, your mental health is as important as your financial fitness when it comes to handling your money and investments. You must feel psychologically at ease with your monetary decisions. The greater the degree of synchronization between your personal style and your investment activities, the greater the likelihood of financial success.

The characteristics of different kinds of investments and money-management approaches vary as do our personality traits.

They relate to one another, often in ways that are unknown to us. To help you fit your personality traits to the form of investment, consult the chart on pages 184-188. Before you begin, however, evaluate your financial-management plan to determine exactly how much money you may "sanely" direct toward investment ventures. Do not overcommit yourself.

Also bear in mind that the investment markets are certainly not everybody's cup of tea. Only about 20 percent of the public are involved in the stock market. However, it is also true that many people leave their money in savings accounts at notoriously low interest rates. One executive left $250,000 in a savings account because he had not gotten around to putting the money where it could work for him. To keep up with or surpass inflation, and to take full tax advantage of dividends and capital gains, you need to turn to more aggressive forms of investment.

As you review the chart that follows, remember that the investment strategies are *suggestions* for you to think about and discuss with professional advisors. The purpose here is to relate your psychological profile to your financial profile so you can maximize your money-handling abilities and decisions.

As you think about your investment preferences, be aware that it is impossible to meet all your needs with one investment. Most people are concerned about the safety of the principal of their investment, the potential tax advantages, and the amount of cash that will be generated from the money they invest. These are, however, not their only thoughts on the matter.

Wherever you invest, consider the debt you are incurring, the risk you are assuming, and the possible returns you can expect. You also need to know yourself well enough to assess whether you are likely to involve yourself directly in the management of your investment, or whether you will leave it to your financial advisors. You must also, of course, decide how much liquidity you require and how likely it is that you will need to obtain funds rapidly.

There are many personality features that relate to investment choices and strategies. The main factors are outlined in the chart. The left-hand column lists personality traits, the center column outlines financial behavior that goes with each personality trait, and the right-hand column suggests investments that are suitable to that personality trait and, in some cases, those that are not suitable.

Choosing Your Investment Strategy

Personality Traits	Financial Behavior	Investment Strategies
I like to take risks.	I like to take chances for potential high yield.	Most Suitable: • Futures • Options • Commodities • Junior stocks • Own business • Tax shelters Least Suitable: • T Bills • Bank deposits
I hate to take risks.	I prefer conservative choices and safe bets.	Most Suitable: • T Bills • Term deposits • Government bonds Least Suitable: • Commodities • Futures • Junior stocks • Options • Tax shelters • Own business

(continued on next page)

Personality Traits	Financial Behavior	Investment Strategies
I cannot admit mistakes (to myself or others) and I cannot accept losses.	I may "ride losers" too long and hold on to losing investments past a reasonable point.	Most Suitable: • Mutual funds • Real estate • Convertible debentures • T bills • Savings bonds Least Suitable: • Any speculative ventures • Junior stocks
I can make decisions and use sound judgment.	I carefully weigh choices, then I make a solid decision and stick with it.	Most Suitable: • Any well-researched investment opportunity • Own business • Tax shelters Least Suitable: • "Hot tips" and trendy investments • Investments requiring quick decisions
I can keep stress levels manageable and in the productive range.	I can avoid "white knuckles" and going past the "pillow point" (anxiety reactions to worry regarding losing money).	Most Suitable: • Common shares • Mutual funds • Real estate • T Bills • Government bonds Least Suitable: • Commodities • Futures • Junior stocks

(continued on next page)

Personality Traits	Financial Behavior	Investment Strategies
I am tolerant of ambiguity and unpredictability. I can accept financial situations that are subject to much change.	I can live with financial uncertainty.	Most Suitable: • Own business • Common stocks • Mutual funds • Options • Futures Least Suitable: • T Bills • Government bonds
I can wait for gratification. I am rarely impulsive.	I don't mind waiting for my capital to build. I'm not in a hurry to make money.	Most Suitable: • Blue chip common stocks • Real estate • Mutual funds • T Bills • Savings bonds Least Suitable: • Options • Tax shelters
I cannot wait for gratification. I tend to be impulsive.	I make investments for quick rewards.	Most Suitable: • Options • Futures • Rights and warrants • Bonds on margin • Tax shelters • Junior stock issues Least Suitable: • Mutual funds • T bills • Real estate • Preferred stocks

(continued on next page)

Personality Traits	Financial Behavior	Investment Strategies
I tend to follow cues from inside myself. I am a leader.	I don't follow the investment herd. I am independent in my financial transactions.	Most Suitable: • Index options • Financial futures • T Bills • Warrants • Stocks • Own business Least Suitable: • Trendy investments
I tend to follow cues from others. I am a follower.	I prefer to invest as others do. I don't like acting on my own.	Most Suitable: • Mutual funds • T Bills • Savings bonds • Real estate Least Suitable: • Options • Futures
I like to feel powerful and important.	I make investment decisions to increase my feelings of power and authority and to enhance my status in other people's eyes.	Most Suitable: • Common shares • Rights • Warrants • Tax shelters • Real estate • Own business • Gold and silver • Art and collectibles Least Suitable: • T Bills • Bonds • Preferred stocks

(continued on next page)

Personality Traits	Financial Behavior	Investment Strategies
I enjoy a feeling of achievement or accomplishment.	I choose investments that enhance my sense of concrete achievement.	Most Suitable: • Sole proprietor in service industry • Common shares • Regular savings plan Least Suitable: • Options • Futures • Preferred stocks

Your Financial Life Plan

Timing is also an important consideration in your investment planning. What we invest, when we invest, and how we invest our money: the answers to these questions in part depend on the life phase we are in. For example, a person in her mid-twenties—having few available funds and seeking to build equity over time—might put her available financial resources in money-market funds and short-term certificates. An investor in his mid-thirties might explore the stock market, keeping in mind the financial demands of raising a family, if he has one, and of paying the mortgage, along with other family-related expenses.

Liquidity is an important consideration to people in their twenties and thirties, because they might need to convert investments into ready cash. Stocks, bonds, certificates, money-market funds, and some mutual funds would qualify for liquidity readiness.

A person in her forties who has established a pretty secure financial base may wish to expand into more speculative directions. She must, however, be prepared to lose the money—if it goes that way—without becoming distraught.

An individual in his fifties must watch his funds very carefully as he prepares for retirement. Safety in his savings is very important, as is the wise maintenance of existing investments. Secure fiscal vehicles like short-term certificates, Treasury bills, and government bonds are the kind of investments that can safely be entered into at this stage.

As a person nears retirement, her earning pattern will probably not change much, and there will be little income growth. She should plan carefully for the loss of her regular income, and make every effort to arrange her financial assets so that they are flexible enough to keep pace with inflation. Short-term investments that keep pace with ongoing interest rates are better than fixed-rate investments.

Sane Investments

Sane investment practice calls upon your ability to assess the role of your emotions. Fear, envy, and greed can seriously interfere with successful investing. Green Therapies can help you overcome your sore spots in this area.

Important psychological factors for you to consider about yourself as an investor include:

- your degree of rigidity and flexibility (are you willing to admit to mistakes or to take a loss?);
- your relative degree of impulsiveness versus your self-control (do you tend to sell winners too quickly? are you unable to let go when it is in your best interests to do so?);
- your ability to make choices (do you have difficulties making choices and decisions in your life in general and in money matters in particular?);
- your expectations (do you expect to make a killing or just a reasonable profit?).

In addition to these vital elements, you must also develop and maintain realistic hopes and a healthy capacity to deal with disappointments and reversals. Here are some tips to help you be a better and more sane investor:

Tip 1: Work out a lifetime "curriculum" into which you can fit your investment goals and from which you can assess whether you are attaining them. If not, you can revise the goals or the curriculum.

Tip 2:   Be absolutely realistic about risk when it comes to investments. Do not invest money in ways that will make you highly anxious and insecure (the "white knuckle" syndrome).

Tip 3:   Make sure you have a minimum amount saved—three to six months' total expense—before you make any investments.

Tip 4:   In planning investment strategies, always think in terms of after-tax dollars and your overall tax situation. Get expert input.

Tip 5:   Before you invest any money, you should attend to the following projects: get rid of debts (non-tax-deductible), start a savings program, buy a home (if it fits your lifestyle and budget), initiate a tax-planning program, plan for your children's education, open tax-deferred plans for retirement, look after your will, and buy insurance. Remember also to increase your net worth yearly by a predetermined percentage such as 5, 10, 15, or 20 percent, depending on income, age, and life circumstances.

Tip 6:   In general, start your portfolio gradually and safely with government bonds, term deposits, and Treasury bills and progress up the risk ladder—if this suits you—to mutual funds, stocks and bonds, real estate, mortgages, tax shelters, commodities, and art and collectibles.

Tip 7:   Remember that if you have financial responsibilities other than to yourself, your investments should never jeopardize your family's personal comfort. It is not a very romantic concept, but you should spend only the amount of money that won't be missed, that you won't think about if it's not around and that, if need be, you can kiss goodbye for good.

Tip 8: In that portion of your portfolio where your concern is with liquidity, you should stay away from limited partnerships and land and tax-shelter deals.

Tip 9: In all instances, financial planning, goals, and decisions should support your other goals in life. Intelligent investment decisions depend on knowing what you want in life and what you're willing to pay for it.

Tip 10: Life in general is a trade-off. Investments are no exception—particularly stocks. If you want to have safety, you have to give up the hope of getting rich. If you want to become very rich, you have to be prepared for big risks. Therefore, decide first on your priorities: safety or large gains.

Tip 11: After deciding on your priorities, review the past history and the future prospects of various industries. Get advice from a professional you trust before you purchase anything.

Tip 12: You never know when antiques and collectibles may turn out to be a good investment. For example, Charlie Chaplin's legendary Little Tramp screen props—his hat and cane—were sold recently at a London auction for $22,500. While you can't rely on these kinds of investments to put bread on your table, with the proper knowledge, instincts, and some additional cash, you may make some extra money.

Tip 13: Select an investment advisor (stockbroker, financial planner) only after you have interviewed at least three prospects.

Tip 14: Before you visit a prospective advisor, gather the following information: your net-worth statements, the amount in your emergency fund, your salary, current and expected, the amount you can save monthly, your potential inheritance money, and a list of your financial goals.

Tip 15: When considering making investments, ask yourself how much risk you are willing to take, what financial returns you are expecting, how long you are willing to wait, and how much time you are willing and able to devote to the process.

Tip 16: Your investment objectives should combine the following: income potential, growth possibilities, liquidity factors, and overall safety.

Tip 17: Always work toward a balanced portfolio with the collaboration of your investment advisor. Be sure to consider carefully the role of investment diversification.

Tip 18: To achieve a sane working relationship with your investment counselor, establish a rapport that includes good communication, access to one another, and mutual respect.

Tip 19: The best safeguard for your financial investments is your own personal involvement.

Tip 20: Be prepared to wait for results. Learn to extend your capacity for doing so, and consult the Green Therapies if you need help.

Chapter 21
Credit Cards, Credit Ratings, and Your Fantasy Life

Credit buying is a prime way people can reveal themselves as money misfits—by overdoing it, underdoing it, or not doing it at all. These choices are frequently inefficient and self-defeating attempts to satisfy needs.

Understanding how and why we misuse credit is a necessary but not sufficient precondition of using credit correctly. We must also believe it is possible to change our ways by altering our decision-making behavior, and we must be motivated to change.

Credit abuse has been around since at least three thousand years before Christ—as have efforts like the famous Babylonian Code of Hammurabi (c. 1800 B.C.) to regulate it. In the old days, creditors were protected by pledges or sureties made by the borrower. Pledges, something like collateral today, could include any property, real or personal: land, homes, utensils, and even doors (they were rare and valuable). It could also mean the borrower's wife, concubine, children, or slaves. Times sure have changed!

Many people don't look kindly on the use of credit. For them it goes against the grain of a homespun ideology that says: "Neither a borrower nor a lender be." For others, credit buying—particularly with credit cards—is one of the greatest joys of modern life, and for some of them it has become a bona fide psychological problem.

A Case History: Phyllis

One member of that group was Phyllis. She came to see me because of a problem she was having with lateness. As hard as she tried she was always behind schedule for work, for meetings, and for social events.

Phyllis had been married three times, and was now a single parent, and the sometimes-dejected mother of twin boys eight years of age.

As part of my initial interview, I asked Phyllis to fill out a questionnaire, part of which explored her money habits and attitudes. It turned out that she was as late paying her bills as she was at other things and that she used credit cards to excess.

Phyllis came from a family of eight. Her father, who was cold and emotionally removed from his children, spent much of his time becoming a business success. Phyllis's mother, who was also busy building her own career, attempted to allay the guilt feelings she had about being away from home as much as she was by overindulging her children, particularly her favorite daughter, Phyllis, with money and gifts. The mother was trying to assuage her conscience by substituting things for affection. This factor of overcompensation is often found in the personal histories of problem spenders.

When Phyllis reached adulthood and discovered the magic of credit cards, she became an immediate and permanent devotee and slave to charge-account buying. Phyllis got a greater charge out of charging it than out of spending cash for the same purposes. She liked the sense of an almost infinite spending power, and the joy, as empty as it was at its roots, lay with the act of buying rather than acquiring things. Using a major "love card" made her feel worthwhile. Phyllis could have served for the classic textbook case of the person who tries to purchase love and affection.

Knowing the how and why of Phyllis's problem helped me formulate a plan to help her. We worked on increasing her awareness of how she unwittingly tried to supply what she felt was missing in her life through credit spending.

She began to learn that she could gain a sense of self-love and worth through more productive channels than excessive creditcard purchases and overspending. One of the techniques I used with Phyllis was the Looking Forward Calendar (see page 103), which is particularly useful with people who feel a strong need for emotional nurturance and a steady sense of being cared about. This simple device can be a very effective tool to lift one's spirits and mood. Other Green Therapies were used to assist Phyllis, including Imagery and Letting Go. Interestingly enough, Phyllis improved both her tendency to be late and her credit-buying habits at the same time.

The Credit Experience

Modern life as we know it could not continue without credit, but for many people—such as Phyllis—it can't continue with it. These people have learned to use credit to compensate for what's missing in their lives. If I can't feel better on my own, the rationale goes, then I'll use credit to help me out.

To the misfortune of many, the two-by-four-inch polymer wafer is capable of inducing the most self-defeating and irrational spending imaginable. I call it the Aladdin Syndrome. Instead of rubbing the old brass lamp, you give your magic card to your creditor, who rubs it back and forth then swiftly calls the local genie bureau to make sure Aladdin still works for you and that he's not overdoing his monetary miracles.

Talk about magical thinking and wish fulfillment—Sigmund would have had a Viennese ball analyzing these plastic feces we carry around in our wallets. With them we can have our gratifications met instantly and have anything we want anywhere in department-store fairylands. They subtly and not-so-subtly encourage us to spend money beyond our means, to purchase more than we need, to fool ourselves into forgetting that we are borrowing money (at extraordinarily unfavorable rates of interest), to feed our neurotic compulsions, to build a hand-to-mouth mentality, and generally to disregard sound financial and personal management practices. Plastic money may be more dangerous than paper money to the misuser.

A Case History: Ray

Ray certainly suffered from the toxic effects of abuse—of both money and alcohol. When we first met he was thirty-nine, an unmarried, art-loving dilettante with an appetite for people, food, drink, and the creative media. By profession he was a freelance art director. He collected *objets d'art*, flamboyant clothes, and friends and acquaintances; he spoke to everyone.

In certain respects Ray was narcissistic but the guilt feelings and bouts of self-anger that arose within him often led to masochistic behavior. Typically, he would start out to indulge himself and then end up overindulging others at his own expense—financial and emotional. Debts were the outcome.

I am not sure how he managed to obtain so many credit cards—eight, to be exact—since his employment history was another of his problems. He was a hard and industrious worker but his frequent personality clashes with managers and other authority figures led to several dismissals.

Ray had many parties and entertained beyond his means by using his plastic promissory notes as they were designed to be used—without restraint. When the bills flooded in, so did his depression. At those moments he would forget the fun times and withdraw for days, maybe weeks. Ray's friends didn't come around during these periods and that added to his sense of loss and emptiness.

As we studied Ray's psychohistory, with special reference to the role of money, we learned that he was constantly in competition with his favored younger sister. Ray tried to shine by attracting friends and by luring the attention of others. It worked superficially but often left him with a residual hollow feeling.

Underlying Ray's depression and anger were sadness and fear. He felt like an outsider to his family and desperately wanted to belong, even if it cost him—in addition to his peace of mind—more money than he could afford.

I helped Ray reduce his high levels of stress and increase his understanding of how his behavior was failing to supply what he needed emotionally. Over a period of time he reduced his level of anxiety along with the number of credit cards he owned, and he began to use money more sanely.

Credit Victims

In addition to Phyllis and Ray, Larry Gamble also had a tendency to use his credit card irresponsibly to raise funds. He sometimes ended up losing twice: first the money from wayward wagers, and second the interest on the credit-card loan, neither of which he could afford.

The famous intrigue novelist John Le Carré, author of best-selling books such as *The Spy Who Came in From The Cold*, tells us of his flamboyant and manipulative father, who lived high on the hog for many years. He had charge accounts at the best of London's West End restaurants, a flat in Chelsea, expensive cars, race horses, and custom-made clothing, and he traveled in the grand manner. Le Carré reports that at the time of his father's death:

> Letters, bills and bank statements in red ink, both foreign and domestic, lay ankle deep on the floor. . . . Everyone trying to figure out where all the money had gone. Sound as some of his schemes undoubtedly were . . . there wasn't a bean and my guess is there never had been.

People who need a way to reconcile their internal conflicts about spending money freely and easily and perhaps incurring debt in the process, with the moral and historical injunctions against succumbing to debtor behavior, have found that charging it fits the bill. By using credit cards they give themselves permission to indulge and enjoy a fantasy life—what it would be like to be a big spender and to just sign their names to bills as the rich do.

To some degree we would all like to live a life of luxury and forget about loans and debt. By using plastic money we fool ourselves into forgetting that in reality we're writing our own loans. The power to create funds leads to a very heady feeling indeed. It's not a license to print our own money, but it comes very close!

Credit buying and debt promotion cause a number of money headaches. If you have any of these, follow the suggested Green Therapies. Decide which of the symptoms listed in the left-hand column best describes you. The middle column lists Green Therapies (Chapters 7 to 14) you might try for the Payoffs described at the right.

Curing Your Credit Card Headaches

Symptom	Green Therapy	Payoff
If you feel a strong need to use your credit card when you feel down or depressed, try:	Cognitive Behavior Therapy Psychodynamics (Brief) Psychological Flashcards Destressing and Systematic Relaxation Guided Imagery	You'll have greater self-control in buying situations, and it will be easier for you to avoid using your card.
If you tend to overuse credit cards—by buying things you wouldn't pay cash for or by generously paying restaurant tabs—try:	Cognitive Behavior Therapy Psychodynamics (Brief) Psychological Flashcards Thought Stopping Destressing and Systematic Relaxation	You'll increase your awareness about why you use credit the way you do, and you'll learn how to set realistic limits.
If you get caught up in the addictive aspect of using credit cards, or if you use them to get a high or to impress others, or if you simply have difficulty denying yourself, try:	Destressing and Systematic Relaxation Psychological Flashcards Cognitive Behavior Therapy Guided Imagery	You'll learn to distinguish neurotic motivations from reality-oriented ones. Your ability to recognize self-defeating acts will grow, leading to saner money handling.

(continued on next page)

Symptom	Green Therapy	Payoff
If you try to hide your credit problems, including overuse or improper use of your credit cards, by pretending there's no problem, try:	Psychodynamics Cognitive Behavior Therapy Psychological Flashcards Destressing and Systematic Relaxation Thought Stopping	You'll learn how to acknowledge that there is a problem, and you'll be more willing to do something about it.

The How of Credit

Surely one of the most mellifluous-sounding expressions is: buy now—pay later. Countless millions have joyously taken the advice to heart. Credit is, of course, never having to say you borrow, although that is precisely what you are doing.

Credit, as we are told, is a privilege, and must not be abused. Learning how to use it properly is an important money-management principle to develop.

Start by familiarizing yourself with the basics of personal credit management through the use of good resource material. Inquire at the credit bureau about the best way to establish a credit rating. It has been suggested by some people that one way to go about this is to borrow a modest sum of money from a bank where you have a savings account as collateral. Then pay the loan off quickly and methodically, thereby establishing yourself as a good credit risk.

In recent years increasing attention has been paid to the number of inequalities faced by women seeking credit. It is important for women to establish their own credit ratings and to obtain credit cards in their own names. A married woman in particular should make sure she has a financial identity separate from her husband's.

Paying your credit-card bills fully and on time also establishes an excellent credit rating and gives you a short-term interest-free loan. Financially speaking, this is the ideal arrangement for a sound fiscal policy: you borrow and make your purchase but you avoid any interest charge by paying on time and in full (although some companies are now charging a small transaction fee). The credit-card receipt can also be used for record-keeping purposes.

It is important to think of credit use as icing on the cake, to be enjoyed after all your basic financial needs have been met. Use it as a part of your total money-management philosophy and allow yourself the occasional "fun" purchase. Here are some more tips to help you use credit creditably:

Tip 1: Call your local credit-bureau office and find out how to obtain a copy of your credit rating. If you don't have the highest rating possible, find out what is necessary to bring one about.

Tip 2: Read all the details of credit-card contracts. Familiarize yourself with the actual cost of your credit, and what you should do if your card is lost or stolen.

Tip 3: Keep in your files a careful up-to-date record of all the credit cards you own with the card numbers and expiry dates.

Tip 4: Always pay the full balance payable on the due date. Never use the "minimum payment due" feature. It will cost you a great deal of money in interest. Paying interest fees is the opposite of good money-management practice.

Tip 5: When using your credit card, always be sure the details are properly filled in and then destroy the carbons to eliminate the chance of fraudulent use of your credit-card number. Be sure to take and keep your own copy.

Tip 6: Be very wary of giving your credit-card number on the telephone. There have been incidents in which credit-card numbers were used for fraudulent purposes.

Tip 7: Set a firm limit on your credit spending each month and keep a record of these expenses.

Tip 8: A sound credit rating can be used to great advantage in establishing a line of credit for future business ventures and investment purposes.

Tip 9: Using a credit card to make purchases does not absolve you from following sound buying practices. Remember to comparison shop and to be aware of good value.

Tip 10: Don't make purchases you wouldn't ordinarily make just because you are using a credit card. Ask yourself: Do I need it? Can I afford it? Will I be able to pay for it when the bill arrives?

Tip 11: If your work or investment needs warrant it, consider establishing a line of credit with your bank. This is similar to the line-of-credit limit set on your credit card.

Tip 12: Never forget that if you pay off your credit-card debt on the installment plan, the dinner you bought for forty dollars may eventually end up costing you fifty-five dollars or more, depending on how long it takes you to pay it off. This is negative money management.

Tip 13: If you ever allow debt balances to accrue, never let the total monthly debt payment exceed 15 percent of your monthly income (after all deductions).

Tip 14: In applying for credit, remember that the lender is interested in the three Cs of credit granting: Character (your personal strengths), Capacity (sufficient income to repay), and Capital (overall assets).

Tip 15: Remember the general pros and cons of credit cards.
Pros:
- they are useful in emergencies and for traveling;
- they help you keep track of expenses;
- they offer short-term "free credit";
- they allow you to make major purchases at sale times.

Cons:
- they charge high interest rates;
- they often charge fees;
- they encourage impulse buying and overspending;
- they can contribute to poor money-management practices.

Chapter 22
Living Within Your Means Even If You Have To Borrow To Do So

Shakespeare obviously didn't live in our times. If he had, he never would have advised: "Neither a borrower nor a lender be." We all borrow and we all lend and we couldn't get along otherwise. Neighbors borrow lawn mowers and tools, children borrow toys and games, many of us borrow books, and some of us borrow money.

Borrowing is a way of life. Deficit financing is the way of the world—from the credit still obtained by some people at small neighborhood stores to the elephantine loans made by governments. "Live beyond your means" is almost a motto today. We are encouraged by the buy-now, pay-later mentality. And government overspending also provides a poor model for us to follow.

Some folks believe that borrowing money is bad for their souls. Certain individuals hold that borrowing of any kind isn't good for you. I know someone whose mother informed her at the tender age of eight that she was not to borrow anything from anyone—not even a sheet of paper at school. The mother's reasoning was clear and direct: if her daughter suddenly died having borrowed another child's notepaper, it would be on her account forever in the hereafter!

Borrowing (within certain limits) is neither morally wrong nor neurotic. Nor should it be intimidating. Although some lending institutions may make you feel put down, remember that they exist to lend money and your borrowing is what helps them stay in business.

At one time or another, almost everyone needs to borrow money. Ordinary people who require funds for anything from fence repairing to planned investment feel free to approach lending institutions for the money they need.

Borrow-phobia

Life is different if you have borrow-phobia. As with any other phobia, there is an obsessive, persistent, unrealistic, and intense fear associated with a particular object or situation. In this case, the situation is borrowing money. Consciously, you may recognize the circumstances as harmless but underneath you're a cauldron of worry.

It is interesting to know that more than two hundred and fifty neurotic phobias have been given names in psychiatric practice. They take many forms, ranging from nosophobia (fear of disease) and acrophobia (fear of heights) to chrematophobia (fear of money) and hematophobia (fear of blood).

Borrow-phobia may not have a formal name but it exists nonetheless. Symptoms of borrow-phobia are physical and psychological and they are enough to keep you out of banks for life. Does the very thought of accepting money on your signature alone result in palpitations, perspiration, nausea, and even tremors? Do you wonder if you need the service of a cardiologist? In reality it's another part of your anatomy that needs sorting out.

The Sane Borrower Test

Answer the following questions yes or no.
1. Do you believe that borrowing money is wrong?
2. When you borrow money do you use it for many different purposes at one time?
3. Do you borrow to pay your bills at the end of the month?
4. Do you spend more than 15 percent of your monthly income, after deductions, to pay off debts?
5. Do you use your credit card to buy beyond your means?
6. Do you tend to buy things with your credit card that you wouldn't have paid cash for?
7. When you borrow money do you take the first loan rate offered?
8. Do you buy now and pay later?

9. Do you have the urge to show off by using your credit card even when it's beyond your means?
10. Do you borrow whenever you're short of cash?

If you answered no eight or more times, you are a very sane borrower. If you answered no five or more times, you are an okay borrower but you can use some advice on healthy borrowing. If you answered no three or fewer times, you are likely to end up in debtors' prison.

A Case History: Mark

Consider Mark's dilemma. Mark was a thirty-three-year-old up-and-coming architect who had struggled hard to get where he was. He had two children and a supportive wife who helped to keep their lives on an even keel. The boat started to rock when Mark saw an opportunity to start his own consulting firm.

He did some research and found out that it would cost him about fifty thousand dollars to get things going. Then he began to explore ways to obtain the funds. As soon as he started to think about borrowing the money he felt faint and fatigued and he began to experience some panic. He had a thorough physical examination by his doctor, who found nothing medically wrong. It was then that we got together to explore another kind of help—counseling.

Mark had associated borrowing money with strong feelings of dependency, which he couldn't accept. The very thought of owing someone money, especially a large sum, made him recall the times in his life when he borrowed heavily to complete his schooling. He worried, he was angry, he was fearful. He didn't like to be at the mercy of a money lender.

The fears he was experiencing were irrational. As with many phobias, the consciously identified source of the fear masks the real fear. In Mark's situation the consciously identified fear was his anxiety about being dependent. The masked fear had to do with guilt toward his father.

Mark's parents fought over money, over assertiveness, and over careers. Mark's mother felt that her husband was too dependent on his parents for financial support. She urged him to get financial backing from other business sources. She felt he was too tied to his parents. He, however, insisted he didn't want to borrow the money elsewhere.

As Mark grew older he came to side with his mother more and more, but he loved his father and felt guilty about his disloyalty. He grew increasingly anxious when the issue of borrowing money arose between his parents.

When he went to school, his friends would comment on his exaggerated aversion to borrowing small sums of money. They commonly borrowed money from each other for a ride or candy. Mark would do without rather than accept a loan.

He continued to avoid borrowing until he was forced to do so to pay for his education. The anxiety that that loan caused encouraged him again to stay out of debt—which he did until the consulting-firm opportunity arose. Then all the old neurotic anxiety returned. This illustrated another common feature of the phobic fear: it persists long after any serious threat has disappeared.

Mark's phobic reaction to borrowing stemmed from his unconscious feelings of guilt toward his father. He had, in effect, taken on some of his father's feelings of personal uncertainty and self-doubt, and those ended up affecting his self-confidence.

To overcome his fears Mark needed to have repeated successes in the area of borrowing and dealings with lenders. These were crucial to help him overcome the negative conditioning to which he had been exposed.

Mark was aided by the process of Deconditioning, a combination of Destressing and Systematic Relaxation and Guided Imagery. Mark was told, for example, to imagine himself discussing a loan for his planned business with a banker. He worked out a list of similar situations, which ranged from least anxiety arousing to most. As he practiced imagining the items on the list, he applied relaxation techniques. Eventually he was able to control his fear well enough to borrow the money he needed.

An important element in overcoming phobias is the complete

Living Within Your Means Even if You Have to Borrow to Do So 207

support of those close to the phobic person. In this case, Mark's wife, Ann, was very understanding and encouraging.

Borrow-phobia may take many different forms, some obvious and others subtle. Whatever the unconscious root causes, the effects are the same: the thought of borrowing and paying back money causes some people to malfunction and sets the stage for financial inefficiency.

Banks

Banks have been around longer than you think. There is evidence that the temples of Babylon made loans four thousand years ago and that private commercial-banking firms were in existence around the year 575 B.C. Could you imagine, for example, Socrates opening a super-interest savings account or Plato meeting with the loans officer to get an ideal loan?

Ancient banks used different kinds of legal tender. Psychologist Henry Lindgren reports: "The Egyptians under the Ptolemies developed a sophisticated system of banking based on units of grain. Bank headquarters were in Alexandria; farmers could deposit wheat in one of the branch banks and issue checks that were negotiable—i.e., that would be honored by any governmental granary."

Author and money-management expert Martin Meyer informs us that the real ancestors of our contemporary bankers were the English goldsmiths who flourished from the twelfth to the fourteenth centuries. These merchants held people's gold and specie (solid gold and silver coins) for safekeeping for which they were paid a fee. They in turn issued notes to the depositors for the precious metals they held.

By the fourteenth century, temptation got the best of the goldsmiths and they started to issue notes in excess of the real value of the gold supply they held. This conversion of their roles from custodians of the gold to lenders of funds owned by other people made them the first modern commercial bankers. Some say it was downhill from that point on.

For certain individuals, a sense of wariness and banks have always gone together. Do you remember the wonderful short story called "My Financial Career" by Stephen Leacock? It totally captures the experience of the little guy who feels displaced in the mausoleum-like halls of a banking institution. The story begins: "When I go into a bank I get rattled. The clerks rattle me; the wickets rattle me; the sight of the money rattles me; everything rattles me. The moment I cross the threshold of a bank and attempt to transact business there, I become an irresponsible idiot."

The appeal of Leacock's story comes from the universality of the experience he describes. Banks make a lot of us feel about as high as the lowest rung on a ladder. It's as if we had drunk the leftover from the "Drink Me" bottle in *Alice in Wonderland*.

Why do people feel threatened in banks? Well, banks are built to make us feel small. The structure and design of savings-and-loan institutions emphasize the unequal power relationship between the customer and the bank. They have all the money; they have the shiny steel vaults and sophisticated alarm systems and ominous security equipment. They clearly mean business, and we often feel intimidated by them.

Bank Paranoia: The Fear and Avoidance of Lending Institutions

Bank paranoiacs are easy to spot. As soon as they near a bank they start looking over their shoulders, and then they worry that their nervous behavior is being observed and will be interpreted negatively. Many of them will become apoplectic about any money negotiation, but borrowing is at the top of the list.

These people secretly fear the revival of debtors' prisons.

Punishment for nonpayment is one of the secret terrors of would-be borrowers. What terrible fate might befall them if, for some unexplained reason, they fail to return what was lent to them, with interest? This kind of reaction is neurotic to be sure, but it is as potent as if it were the gospel truth. On some subliminal level, the fear of consequences is partly responsible for some people's fears of incurring debt.

People who are intimidated by banks and loans have other concerns as well. They are anxious about the prospects of losing their possessions when they sign notes of collateral. They are convinced that banks have an extraordinarily wide latitude in collecting unpaid debts.

There is indeed a rational concern at work here. There is no question that if you incur financial indebtedness you are required to dissolve the debt. Concerns about one's ability to fulfill that responsibility are normal. But some people's fears are exaggerated, and these attitudes often oppose their best interests since in many instances it is sensible and beneficial to borrow funds.

Why Are People Afraid To Borrow?

Fear is a scary subject. People don't like to talk about it, especially when it concerns money. So far, the apprehensions about borrowing funds we've looked at have stemmed from fears of feeling dependent, of punishment, and of loss. Alas, there are others as well.

Handling dollars, particularly large sums, makes excessive money worriers uncomfortable. Their anxiety levels and blood pressure can rise precipitously if they just contemplate high finances. In many cases these fears can be traced to attitudes learned in childhood.

Everything we know about money we've learned. If money comes to be associated, for example, with thoughts of distrust, conflict, and hard times, it isn't hard to see why we might avoid monetary matters.

A Case History: Susan

Susan's parents distorted her attitudes toward money for her entire life. They didn't intend to do so, of course, but that's the way it worked out. At all the emotional crossroads in her life, money was at issue. Her parents fought and argued all the way to the bank. If Susan's mother and father were yelling, there was a 98 percent chance that it was about finances. They disagreed about spending, saving, investing, and even giving their money away to charity. Susan knew about fiscal matters in her family whether she chose to or not. Even when her father wanted to borrow money it generated conflict in the family, which she felt.

Susan learned to connect discord and bad feelings with cash flow. For many years she tried to pretend that money didn't exist, but that didn't work.

Not surprisingly, her attitudes affected her marriage. When her husband, Mike, asked her to manage the bill-paying for the family, all her old bitter memories came cascading back. In going over the family budget, she found out the details of loans Mike had taken out. She had known they had borrowed money but seeing the figures threw her back to her childhood days with her parents.

Mike couldn't understand why Susan was so upset and why she was unable to stop crying for an hour. When he found out what was wrong, he suggested that she go for counseling.

Susan had come to view money as a source of alienation between people. She perceived it as interfering with relationships and perhaps preventing their success. She was afraid of losing Mike's love. For her, affections and money issues had gotten all mixed up. Learning about the loans frightened her and heightened her sense that she wasn't in control.

When Mike asked Susan to look after their fiscal affairs, Susan felt angry at him. She had projected her father's behavior onto Mike, and she felt unconsciously that her husband was looking for a fight. Why else would he confront her with this money obligation? Susan found herself holding a grudge against Mike and blaming him for how she felt. She was unwilling to accept responsibility for it herself.

These feelings were the residue of old unresolved conflicts. Susan's memories contained a lot of suffering when it came to money matters. Borrowing, in particular, made her feel vulnerable.

Here's how we dealt with it in therapy:

Susan: I don't know why I get so angry with Mike. Inside I know it's not his fault but at times I can't control my

	hostility. Thinking about doing the books and the loans really upsets me.
NF:	Tell me what you thought about, Susan, when Mike asked you to do the household books.
Susan:	At first I cried. I think that happened because I saw my life repeating itself before my eyes. I couldn't stop it from happening and it scared me. I really believed I couldn't control it. For some reason, owing money scared me. I thought: What if we can't pay it back?
NF:	So as we explore behind the scenes the drama gets clearer. Your whole sense of emotional safety was jolted. You began to fear a loss of control over your own life in relation to money issues. Sometimes people become frightened that they're going to go crazy at those times.
Susan:	That's it exactly. I really worried about my sanity. Not for long, just long enough to feel really scared.
NF:	Well, Susan, we've been exploring some of the dynamics of your life. We've probed into the background of your negative feelings about money. You understand better the role that your parents played and particularly how you began to identify Mike with your father. You saw dollars as dividing people. And today, when you think about borrowing, you worry. How would you ideally like to see your situation resolved?
Susan:	Well, I suppose I would want to be more at ease and relaxed about the whole business of money. After all, it's only colored paper, come to think of it. I'm a little surprised that I'm thinking about it so lightly.
NF:	Susan, what you're talking about is achieving a sense of resolution and peace. You've been carrying around this attitude of blame and resentment toward your family—mainly your father. That's the first thing you have to understand.
Susan:	I see that a lot more clearly. I also haven't really been accepting the responsibility for my feelings.
NF:	That's true. It's important to realize that you do have a lot more control over your actions and feelings than you think. One of the main ways of coming to terms

	with your concerns here is to understand that you've been holding your feelings of fear and blame for so long. It's essential that you begin to forgive people in your life for the wrongs you hold against them.
Susan:	You mean forgive my parents for their negative influences on me? Forgive them for the fact that a lot of my discomfort and anxiety is set off by money responsibilities such as paying off loans?
NF:	Yes. And also forgive yourself. Stop thinking about blame. When things go wrong in our lives, we often find it convenient to find fault with someone or something. We direct our anger that way. And we can then feel like a victim in the drama, and adopt a woe-is-me attitude toward the world.
Susan:	It's true—and I also feel quite sorry for myself.
NF:	We're talking here about changing your attitudes. If you believe you can't change things, they will definitely not change. You have to be willing to change for the better and to let go of the old negative views.
Susan:	I think I know what you mean, but how do I do it?
NF:	There's nothing magical about it. It takes time and it has to become a growing part of you. In concrete terms, you should take on the money-handling job and confront your anxieties as they arise, much as you would deal with imaginary bugbears in a dark room. Put the light on whenever you find yourself in the dark about your money fears. Then you'll discover there's really nothing there to fear. You must distinguish facts from false impressions. It's a fact that you must repay money borrowed, but it's a false impression that it is overwhelming and that you won't be able to handle it successfully.

Susan and I continued to work together for four months on her monetary anxieties, after which she began to feel more at ease. She gradually took on more of the responsibilities for money management in her family, and her confidence increased over time. Our counseling sessions finally ended when Susan and Mike agreed that the quality of their financial lives had improved dramatically.

The Psychological Reasons For Borrowing

We borrow cash to fill a void. Something is empty and we feel a need to replenish it. We want a bigger house, some stocks, more clothes, more education, a stereo system, a summer cottage, or some real estate. If we acquire these things we believe we will feel psychologically more complete. Life will be better.

In some respects these feelings are accurate. If borrowing is safe, there is nothing wrong with it. In fact, many of us would never be able to enjoy some of the material pleasures like a home without fiscal aid. What is to be avoided at all costs is buying into the neurotic money game.

For many of us money is associated with our personal safety and our self-esteem. We think that if we have more money, even if we have to borrow it, we will gain more emotional comfort and status. In this way we buy a sense of power and superiority.

Changes in our monetary situation are experienced as changes in ourselves. Because we identify with our money, an insufficient amount of it causes us to become anxious and to feel inadequate. At these times we are like children; we tell ourselves stories to comfort ourselves. A common tale we spin is that if we increase our cash flow even slightly we will float. Here's Henry Lindgren on the a-little-more-money delusion: "The belief that 'a little more money' will solve one's problems is a delusion, but it is one that is cherished by almost everyone. Some people deal with the problem of the 'need for a little more money' by borrowing on their home or personal property and sinking deeper into debt." The point here, of course, is that the a-little-more-money idea is a myth.

Now that you understand some of the psychology of borrowing, you can decide if your attitudes are holding you back. Does borrowing present conflicts or anxieties in your life?

Decide which of the symptoms listed in the left-hand column

best describes you. The middle column lists the Green Therapies (Chapters 7 to 14) you might try for the Payoffs described at the right.

Curing Your Borrowing Headache

Symptoms	Green Therapy	Payoff
If you tend to worry about—or fear—the idea of borrowing, or if dealing with forms, applications, and loans officers arouses your anxiety try:	Psychodynamics Cognitive Behavior Therapy Psychological Flashcards Destressing and Systematic Relaxation Thought Stopping Guided Imagery	You'll feel more comfortable about the idea of borrowing money, and you'll be able to go through the necessary steps to obtain a loan.
If you over-borrow and are a poor financial planner, try:	Cognitive Behavior Therapy Psychodynamics (Brief) Destressing and Systematic Relaxation Psychological Flashcards	You'll get a clearer picture of the role of borrowing in overall financial-management planning.
If you're apprehensive about repaying loans and think about the consequences of default, or if you're afraid to deal with large sums, try:	Cognitive Behavior Therapy Psychodynamics (Brief) Destressing and Systematic Relaxation Thought Stopping Letting Go	You'll be considerably more relaxed about your ability to pay off a debt.

(continued on next page)

Symptoms	Green Therapy	Payoff
If you were taught that borrowing is evil and you still think it's wrong, try:	Cognitive Behavior Therapy Psychodynamics (Brief) Thought Stopping Letting Go Guided Imagery	With help from the people around you, you'll be able to change your old attitudes.

The How of Borrowing

The idea of paying a loan back in specific monthly installments over a fixed period of time is only seventy years old. It was devised by an enterprising man named Arthur Morris in 1916 as a way for working people to borrow money from banks and other lending institutions. The Morris Plan is responsible for most of the popular approaches to borrowing money in our day.

Borrowing today is a much more sophisticated business than it was back in Morris's time, but like all monetary matters in our lives, it should ideally fit into an overall financial-management scheme rather than being left to haphazard or spontaneous decisions.

Before you apply for a loan, here are some points you should consider:
- Are you able and willing to repay it?
- What are you borrowing for?
- Could you do without it? If not, why not?
- What are your attitudes toward borrowing? Are you comfortable with the idea?
- Have you thought of other ways to solve the problem? For example, deferring the purchase, raising money in other ways, or borrowing from friends or family?

Borrowing reveals our priorities and our values in life. If you value living in a responsible manner, then your decision to borrow money will be tempered by careful thought and a realistic evaluation of your financial fitness and your ability to eliminate your debt as quickly as possible.

If you still feel uncomfortable about borrowing, remember that it calls into play your sense of trust, of personal integrity, and of responsibility. If you feel the psychological aspects are causing you problems, consult the Green Therapies.

When you are ready to get your loan, make sure you visit a few banking and financial institutions before you decide which is best for you. Go in looking and feeling confident, clear-minded, and decisive. Have all your personal information (income, expenses, budget, a list of assets and liabilities) concisely summarized for your potential lender. If you're married, take your spouse along; borrowing is a family affair.

When you check out the different loan sources, be sure to compare them carefully. Here are some questions:
- Are there different repayment programs available and what are they?
- Do you need collateral?
- Is a co-signer necessary?
- What is the annual percentage rate of interest on the loan?
- What is the total cost of interest for the life of the loan?
- What are the late charges?
- Is there a penalty for paying off the loan early? If so, how much is it?

With all this information at hand, you'll be in a better position to get the best loan possible and to feel in control of the situation. Here are some more tips to help you borrow sensibly:

Tip 1: Decide how much you can borrow and under what circumstances. Review your total income, monthly expenses, assets, liabilities, and budget as well as your overall financial plan.

Tip 2: The ideal time to find out what is involved in borrowing is well before you need the loan. As part of your money-management arrangements, meet with your bank manager to establish your ability to borrow and to discuss all aspects of applying for a loan.

Tip 3: Shop around for the best borrowing conditions you can find. Obtain the most favorable interest rates and the most suitable and economic repayment plan available. Use whatever bargaining clout you have. If, for example, you have good collateral, an excellent credit rating, and a splendid loan-repayment history, you may get a better deal.

Tip 4: Always check all the terms of the loan carefully. Be alert for hidden costs, such as an insurance premium or search fees or legal fees. Ask questions and get answers about these matters.

Tip 5: Make sure you are sensible about the monthly repayment schedule. Do not enter into a loan that will force you to alter your lifestyle in any significant way unless it is out of dire necessity. If you do, not only are you more likely to fall behind on your payment but you may find you resent the loan and the position it has put you in.

Tip 6: Make every effort to get the interest compounded as infrequently as possible—annually if possible—over the course of the year. This will save you money.

Tip 7: Arrange for as short a repayment plan on the loan as possible. If you choose a long repayment term, thinking that you will actually pay it off early, think again. It ends up costing you more that way.

Tip 8: Be sure to share the details of the loan with your spouse and children (appropriate to their ages). It's an excellent opportunity to help your children learn about the mechanics of borrowing money.

Tip 9: Be absolutely certain to have your lawyer and accountant look over the loan arrangement before you sign the papers, particularly if you are borrowing what you consider to be a substantial sum of money.

Tip 10: Always be aware of the possible tax implications. The interest on your loan may be tax-deductible.

Tip 11: Pay back the loans that are not tax-deductible first and fast. The money you save in doing this is yours. As a general rule, try to borrow for investment purposes (as the interest is often tax-deductible) and pay cash for personal items.

Tip 12: Before borrowing from a bank, check out the pros and cons of more economical loans from private sources, family or relatives, insurance policies, credit unions, or trust companies. Always check with the experts (your lawyer, accountant, or financial planner) before signing anything. Always make sure you fully understand the terms and conditions of the loan you obtain.

Tip 13: If you borrow money and the debt could possibly end up being a threat to the well-being of your family or your estate—for example, through unforeseeable default—be sure to get the loan insured. The cost of doing so would be more than worth it.

Tip 14: When you apply for a loan always make sure that your existing credit accounts are up to date. Double check by getting in touch with the credit bureau.

Tip 15: If you can't make your loan payments, don't rush into refinancing installment loans or loan consolidations. Go for debt counseling and avoid expensive financial pitfalls. Most cities have credit-counseling services available. Inquire in your area.

Tip 16: Goods and services are not the only things you can borrow money for. It is less common to borrow funds for investment purposes, but no less important. There is a famous business expression: use other people's money to make money for yourself. Once again, consult the experts.

Tip 17: If you consider borrowing from friends, family, or relatives, make sure it is done on a strictly business basis. Have legal papers drawn up, spelling out the full terms of the loan, and follow them meticulously if you accept the money. Remember, this is not an ordinary debt; there's a relationship riding on it, too.

Chapter 23
Going for the Gold in the Golden Years

Tennessee Williams said, "You can be young without money but you can't be old without it. You've got to be old *with* money because to be old without it is just too awful." Most of us would agree. We worry, even panic, that we will reach retirement without enough money to meet our needs. We have all heard stories about people who suffered indignities, inconveniences, and hardships because their retirement funds were insufficient.

The Fears of Old Age

Human beings as they age seem to tap an unconscious repository of primordial fears about being abandoned, dependent, helpless, and alone. These are conditions we experienced when we were young and we couldn't fend for ourselves, and many of us use money and the power it represents to protect us from feeling the same way as adults. Money becomes our "parents." It protects us from the slings and arrows of the outside world.

As with all neurotic transactions, there is always an element of reality mixed in. There is no question that money is needed to deal with the necessary demands of later life. The problem occurs when we attempt to use it to calm our separation anxieties, our feelings of loss, and our sadness at unwanted changes. The behavioral distortions that result from these irrational attempts lead to a reduction in the quality of lives of the people so bedeviled.

The classic case is the retired individual who consistently deprives himself of pleasure because he is afraid he will run out of money. Often the fear is out of proportion to the actual dangers.

A Case History: Arnold

Arnold's story illustrates some of these themes. Originally from a large city on the west coast, he and his wife had recently moved to the northeastern United States. Their two daughters had left home and happily married, and Arnold was not looking forward to his retirement or to being "put out to pasture," as he sarcastically phrased it.

Arnold had stashed away a fair bit of money from his years as an engineer and from his sound investments. Along with this he expected to receive a handsome pension, plus profit-sharing goodies. Arnold was excellent at his job and his self-esteem was deeply tied in with the recognition he received from his colleagues. For the most part they were not personal friends, only co-workers, but that didn't matter.

There were two basic reasons he didn't want to leave his employment—besides the emotional gratification he was receiving: first, he didn't feel he had enough money, even though his accountant strongly disagreed with him, and second, he believed the emotional distance between him and his wife would be further exacerbated if he were no longer working.

Arnold was cold and distant with Fran, his wife, and he often abused her verbally. He did not give her the emotional support she needed and in general found it hard to relate to her. Fran, a part-time accountant, knew that there was no justification for his financial fears, but she had long since given up trying to convince him. Besides, a sort of alienation of affection had set in between them. Three years earlier, Arnold, in his attempt to "save" everything, including himself, stopped making love to his wife. At times she felt desperate enough to start an affair, and she imagined herself writing one of those witty and clever personal ads, but she never did. In an odd sort of way she and Arnold had some feelings for each other, but most of the things that Arnold did ended up distancing Fran from him.

Arnold fought his impending job release tooth and nail but to no avail—the company had to tighten its financial belt and letting him go was one of the measures they took. It was sheer hell for him at first. He got in Fran's way and criticized her expenditures. Fran soon began to spend less time at home, deepening Arnold's depression. At this point he came to me for help.

Arnold's psychohistory gave me the clues we needed to understand his anxieties and fears about not having enough financial resources. Arnold's parents had divorced when he was six and his sister was nine. He recalled vividly the day his parents sat them both down to tell them they could no longer get along together and they would be separating and eventually divorcing. Arnold had sobbed uncontrollably as he sadly walked back and forth from his father to his mother as if in doing so he could somehow magically weld them back together again. His sister, Elly, in the meantime, dealt with her pain by mentally armoring herself. She became lighthearted and offhanded about the whole matter—almost as though it weren't really happening to her. She joked and laughed much as a child might sing as he goes into a darkened room.

These emotional earthquakes left Arnold shaky and insecure and he began to build defenses to cope with his feelings. As he grew older he developed a hard outer shell and a strong sense of independence. It was as if he were saying, "If I can't depend on others I'll depend on myself." As soon as he could he began working, and by the time he was in his late teens he had a bankroll of eight and a half thousand dollars, of which he felt quite proud.

Despite the money in the bank, Arnold always felt an undercurrent of self-doubt and insecurity. Even though he was outwardly very successful in his career, he never rid himself of the "methodologies" he learned as a child.

His retirement was like a time machine that returned him to the period when his father "let him go." He was a frightened grown-up person caught with his childhood showing.

Arnold and I first worked on a course of graduated Destressing and Systematic Relaxation exercises, followed with Guided Imagery techniques, which enabled him to reduce his bad feelings. He learned to excise his depression by replacing his negative thoughts ("I don't feel good about myself") with self-reassuring, affirmative statements ("I don't have to handle my life the way I did as a child. I want to feel better about me—and I will").

Once Arnold became aware of his actions and their meanings, he began to assume greater control over them and he felt better about his situation. His attitude toward his disposable income became more realistic and he found that he enjoyed spending money. He and Fran were able to talk about their disagreements, and eventually the whole notion of retirement started to take on new meaning for Arnold.

The Meaning of Retirement

Psychologically speaking, retirement is a period for reexamining and summing up one's life, consolidating a philosophy of life, and reevaluating one's direction and purpose. It is also a time of reaffirming spiritual and religious connections, of considering how to pass on the experiences and accomplishments of a lifetime, and of finding new and stimulating challenges.

In our culture, it is customary to think of age sixty-five as demarcating the transition from working to not working. At this time, people are expected magically to renounce their formal work lives. Some feel that they are being ostracized to a no-man's-land and others enjoy it.

Financial matters, which are a concern for everyone at retirement, may be exaggerated further by lifelong money attitudes. Whatever traits characterize a person's early life will tend to become aggravated by advancing age. Retirement-age problems can also be exacerbated by anxieties about old age and death and by the fear of becoming indigent.

Facing Retirement Realistically

To help clear the neurotic underbrush, it is sometimes helpful to fantasize about what would happen if there were too little money at retirement time. Some people express a concern that they won't be able to take care of their needs and will be forced to accept public services. A primary psychodynamic factor here is their almost phobic fear of losing control of their lives and their fate. In their worst fantasy they imagine themselves in the hands of uncaring strangers and unable to escape.

While it may not reveal the whole story, looking at how you handled other changes in you life will probably give you a clue about what to expect when you face retirement. If you are flexible, able to solve problems, and open to alternate and innovative approaches in your life and if you are not afraid of change, you obviously stand a good chance of successfully working through this transition phase. If these things are true, you probably also tend not to use money neurotically to satisfy your needs.

There are, however, further problems in addition to anxieties about dependency, abandonment, and helplessness, fears of loss of control, and worries about insufficient funds. This other set of potential psychological obstacles has to do with unresolved or dormant difficulties within families. These are often marital in nature, sometimes parental. And, not infrequently, people try to use money to quell conflicts and inner discord in these situations.

A Case History: Samantha

Growing up in a family where money was plentiful though not overabundant, Samantha learned to throw cash at anything that aroused anxiety, just as her mother had done before her. She came from a long line of matriarchs, each sufficiently autocratic to end up alone, either through divorce or the death of a spouse. Samantha, a divorcée and a successful clothes designer, had continued this tradition, and at sixty-two she was seriously considering giving up her work.

She had enough money to retire but shortly after she first began to consider it she started to develop panic reactions when she was alone at home. These feelings were not relieved until friends or one of her two sons came to stay with her. At times she would even ask her ex-husband, with whom she was friendly, to keep her company.

We treated Samantha's behavior as a phobic condition brought about by latent fears of being abandoned, uncared for, and not in control of her life. She tried to assuage her feelings by giving parties and expensive gifts to people but these superficial gestures were completely ineffectual. Her problems had to do with her personal psychology and they could not be solved by using her personal bank account. We employed Destressing and Systematic Relaxation and Affirmations to help her through her phobic symptoms.

Fortunately, Samantha's phobic reaction was mild, and she eventually gave it up as she became reassured and in control of her life once again. At that point she decided to work three days a week for a year and devote the remainder of her time to other interests, including writing. After the year was up, she successfully retired.

Retirement can be an exciting and rewarding time. Ideally, what you need are good health, healthy attitudes, and sufficient finances. If you think your attitudes are in need of work, check the following chart. If your financial picture is less than golden, turn to the second part of this chapter.

Decide which of the symptoms listed in the left-hand column best describes you. The middle column lists the Green Therapies (Chapters 7 to 14) you might try for the Payoffs described at the right.

Curing Your Retirement Headaches

Symptoms	Green Therapy	Payoff
If you are afraid of your approaching retirement because you don't want to acknowledge that you're getting old, or if you feel useless because you're not earning money, try:	Cognitive Behavior Therapy Affirmations Psychological Flashcards Thought Stopping Guided Imagery Destressing and Systematic Relaxation	You'll feel more comfortable about the idea of retiring, and about the idea of change in your life.
If you worry about not having enough money to enjoy life after you retire, and fear that you'll lose control of your life, try:	Cognitive Behavior Therapy Thought Stopping Affirmations Guided Imagery Psychological Flashcards Destressing and Systematic Relaxation	You'll be able to appraise your financial position more realistically, and you'll learn how to turn your worries into sound money-management planning.

(continued on next page)

Symptoms	Green Therapy	Payoff
If you are thinking about retirement but you subconsciously resist the idea and keep putting off planning for it, try:	Destressing and Systematic Relaxation Cognitive Behavior Therapy Psychological Flashcards Affirmations Guided Imagery	You'll be more willing to take charge of your own retirement plans.
If you feel depressed after you retire because the reality doesn't match your expectations, try:	Destressing and Systematic Relaxation Guided Imagery Affirmations Cognitive Behavior Therapy Thought Stopping Psychological Flashcards	You'll be aware of your misconceptions and false beliefs, and you'll learn how to replace them with appropriate and suitable attitudes about the role of retirement in your life.

The How of Retirement Finances

All transitions in our lives have a better chance of success when they are planned, and retirement is no exception. Financial planners take the position that if you want to maintain an optimal standard of living after retirement you should start a retirement fund at least twenty to thirty years prior to stopping work. If you start relatively early, it's a good idea to put away approximately 5 to 10 percent of your income toward retirement. If you begin a savings plan relatively late or if you are self-employed, it would be best to set aside 15 to 20 percent of your money for the same purpose.

Whenever you start your planning, keep in mind that one of the main purposes of good financial management is to eliminate your worries about money. The age you retire at depends on a number of factors: your employer's restrictions on age, your general health, your family, your lifestyle, and your financial resources.

The amount of money you need to retire will depend largely on your lifestyle: how you live before retirement and how you would like to live after retirement. If you wish to maintain the same economic level, then clearly your financial resources will have to generate a similar level of income, taking into consideration inflation and taxes in particular.

Keep in mind that with luck many of your present expenses will no longer apply. For example, your mortgage will probably be paid off and your children will likely be on their own. And, of course, any expenses associated with work will no longer apply. Your life may also become more sedentary and as a result, your financial demands may be more modest.

Once you (and your spouse) have worked out your retirement financial needs, you can decide on the fiscal resources you will need. Remember to count in old age or social security payments, any employer pension plans, government pensions, and investment income. It may be difficult to predict the amounts these will pay in the future, but if you make an educated guess, you'll be able to have at least some idea of where you will stand when you're no longer working for your living.

Here are some tips to help you toward a graceful and well-financed retirement:

Tip 1: In working out your retirement budget, refer to the entries in your regular budget. Some expenses (like child care) and sources of income (like salaries) won't apply, but others will. Also consider new expenses (hobbies or travel) and new income sources (pensions).

Tip 2: There is no hard and fast rule to follow when putting retirement money aside. Your best bet is to put away as much as possible, using whatever financial resources you can muster. Consult an expert in the field to help you.

Tip 3: Even if you don't know exactly how much money you will need when you retire, you can approximate it. Let's say you determined that if you retired today you would need $25,000 a year to cover all your expenses. If we assume the rate of inflation will be 7½ percent and that you will retire in twenty-five years, you will need an annual income of $152,450 upon retirement. Bear in mind when estimating how much income you will require that many of your costs will be reduced upon retirement: living expenses, housing, taxes, and so on. And when you figure out how much you will receive from pensions and similar sources, remember to allow for inflation.

Tip 4: Adjust your retirement planning according to your present age. Start your program with government-approved retirement savings plans and add other investments later.

Tip 5: When planning for your retirement, take into account that in order to maintain the lifestyle you want, you will have to arrange your financial affairs (interest income, dividends, annuities, pensions) so that sufficient funds are available for the rest of your life.

Tip 6: Prior to retirement, review your assets and possessions to determine their net value and their net annual cost to you. Also include the yearly income you derive from these sources. Give some thought to selling your vacation cottage or silver tea service.

Tip 7: As you near retirement, determine as closely as possible how much income you would derive from government retirement plans, private pension plans, guaranteed-income supplements, old age or social security payments, spousal allowances where applicable, and any retirement savings plans. Combine this with other sources of income and compare the total with the overall sum you require. If it is insufficient, cut back on your retirement budget or consider ways of supplementing your income.

Tip 8: When you retire, review your insurance policies to make sure your financial coverages are realistic and up-to-date. Also review the financial arrangements in your will to make sure they conform to your wishes.

Tip 9: Speak to your accountant or tax lawyer to assess the tax implications of your retirement. Make certain, for example, that you can get the best after-tax return for your various investments. In general, the object is to create the lowest tax bite possible. Don't create any more taxable income than is necessary.

Tip 10: Make every effort to go into retirement without any debts.

Tip 11: Consider attending pre-retirement sessions offered by your employer or by qualified people at community colleges and other organizations.

Tip 12: Figure out the cost of things you always wanted to do: special projects, gifts to family members, moving elsewhere, and similar ideas. Relate them to your budget and decide which you can afford.

Tip 13: Investigate the whole question of annuities with specialists in the field to see exactly how they can work for you.

Tip 14: All retirement decisions and plans should include your spouse, and all financial calculations should fully consider the needs of both spouses.

Part IV
Prognosis of Your Monetary Health: What You Have Learned and How Far It Can Take You

We have explored the basic monetary headaches and the neurotic behavior that goes along with them. We have examined the Green Therapies and the help they can offer. And we have also explored the monetary stresses of everyday life as well as practical tips to help relieve them.

We now move on to a synthesis and a look at Moneysanity, what it is and how it can enhance your life as a whole as well as your dealings with money.

Chapter 24
Achieving Moneysanity

Money has been called many things, from the "almighty dollar" to "filthy lucre," and it has served every purpose conceivable, from the highest to the lowest. But money itself is neither good nor evil; only the ends we make it serve can be called moral or immoral, constructive or destructive. In the same way, the role money plays in your life can be healthy or unhealthy. As this book has shown, money can be your "inner tormentor" or your "inner mentor." By altering your monetary attitudes, you can learn to handle your money more effectively. By following the insights gleaned from your "inner mentor" (which teaches you the sane uses of money) you can liberate your financial behavior. All the exercises and suggestions in this book have been directed toward the goal of maximizing your relationship with money as your "inner mentor."

Money is a psychological magnet in your life; it attracts emotions and needs to it depending on your past history and experiences. In some cases this can be harmful, as it is, for example, when money has been used as a symbol (for love or power). Then it becomes a tormentor. But when money is used realistically and not neurotically, it can become your mentor.

The transition from "money as tormentor" to "money as mentor" is outlined in the chart on page 235.

Once you achieve Moneysanity, you will be better able to manage and enjoy your money. For many people, financial liberation will mean increased wealth. For others, monetary freedom will allow them to enjoy their friends, families, associates, and their work more. These aims—wealth and enjoyment—are quite compatible and can be attained together.

Barbara is a good example of someone who achieved these aims. For years she had used her money in a self-defeating way. She had been unable to admit her losses ("mistakes") on the stock market to herself or to anyone else.

Moneysanity Transition

FROM	TO
"Money as Inner Tormentor" (neurotic)	*"Money as Inner Mentor" (non-neurotic)*
You use money to impress and influence other people. To feel powerful and to gain status, you flaunt your wealth.	You are comfortable and at ease in the world. You know that power and status come from within.
You amass money as an end in itself. You like to have money for its own sake.	You value money for what it can do. You can distinguish between worldly desires and emotional needs.
You feel anxious, tense, worried, when you think about money.	You are relaxed about money and can think about it in a logical way.
You distrust other people around your money and you suspect that they are trying to take advantage of you.	You are self-confident and have a good self-image. You know your friends like *you*, not your money.
You hoard money in an attempt to protect yourself.	Your desire to save is healthy.
You have trouble controlling your spending and you tend to buy things impulsively. You like to gamble.	You are a good money manager.

Barbara came to understand that letting go of her losses was in her best financial interests. She found out that it did not mean giving up control of her life. On the contrary, by working through her unresolved feelings she began to regain her self-confidence.

Her increasing comfort and security were reflected in her activities with her children and her friends. She became more assertive in her actions and took courses on the management of securities. She eventually became a stockbroker and was extremely successful in building other people's fortunes, as well as her own. Once she began to channel and focus her energies, she accomplished the high money goals she set for herself. She benefited greatly from "fiscal therapy."

Formulating Your Philosophy of Money

We have pinpointed your negative money habits, diagnosed harmful cash-related traits, and eliminated or significantly decreased your dangerous fiscal tendencies. You are a new person, ready for action. Now we must focus on what those actions might be.

To gain the greatest benefits from your increased understanding, start by writing a brief statement of your personal philosophy of money. Here are some questions to consider:
- What does money mean to me?
- What role does money play in my life?
- What are my goals with money?
- Are my overall goals and attitudes in relation to money consistent with my values and beliefs?
- Are there any inconsistencies in these areas? How might I reconcile them?

Healthy financial control means being masters over our money and making it serve our purposes rather than the other way around. It is crucial that we know our purpose and directions.

Formulating Your Money-Management Program

Now that you have formulated a sound philosophy of money and you are sufficiently emotionally liberated to implement it, you need a money-management program. Begin by surveying your current situation. Review your job, career, financial goals, money needs, and fiscal relationships (with spouse, children, family, friends).

Now decide what changes you want to make. You may wish, for example, to rearrange your style of communication about money matters with your spouse or children. Many families would benefit from a move to a more open style of money management. Secrecy, lack of sharing, and working at cross-purposes are counterproductive to healthy monetary attitudes. And yet many husbands fail to inform their wives about investments, and wives sometimes keep surreptitious financial accounts about which their husbands know nothing. These activities are detrimental to trust, which is vital in a relationship.

Another illustration concerns young people. If you wish to nurture fiscal independence in your children, you must share financial issues and responsibilities at a level appropriate to their age. Help them set up a budget as well as a savings and spending plan. Let them in on family discussions about money.

As you alter your fiscal style, continue to use the Green Therapies to facilitate these changes and to revitalize yourself. For example, if you are considering becoming self-employed or an entrepreneur, use Guided Imagery to stimulate your creative fantasy life as it applies to producing capital. The Affirmations would also be quite supportive, as would the Psychological Flashcards.

A Case History: Peter

Peter was a very achievement-oriented person, and his troubled money ideas had been getting in the way of his accomplishments for a long time. He worried that if he built a successful enterprise from the ground up it would not generate enough funds to sustain itself. He was, in fact, terrified that he would repeat his father's experience. His father's failed business had led to bankruptcy, although he recovered remarkably well. Peter's "money as inner tormentor" thoughts created anxiety, tension, and insecurity in him to such a degree that he kept deferring any possible enterprises.

During this period, he went rather aimlessly from job to job without being happy or fulfilled. His needs for personal success were unmet.

In counseling, Peter revealed his nervous feelings about money and his concerns about not contributing sufficiently to the family finances. We worked on Peter's fears, conflicts, and distorted conceptions using the Green Therapies.

Peter made very good progress and in seven months he was considerably more relaxed and at peace with himself. He learned how to let go of his worries. Then he started up his own business, in computer repair and used-equipment sales. The early stages were quite difficult, and at times Peter became apprehensive. We met from time to time to help him surmount these trying moments.

As time went by he relied more and more on the Green Therapies he had learned. Judging from his huge success— high profits and great satisfaction—it was clear that he made gains from his therapy. Peter increased his earnings by 25 percent over his early years, and he opened a second store in a busy section of the city. He had truly found himself.

Setting Your Goals

To change, you must be goal-oriented and use a "goal-gradient approach." First you set your money goal and then you break it down into smaller goals, which, when gradually completed, bring you to your financial destination.

For example, if your goal is to set up a budget program, organize some small goals to get there. Create an efficient filing system so that all your necessary papers and records are immediately available. Obtain budget outlines from financial-planning books or copy the one in this book (see page 121-22). Prepare a financial overview that includes a statement of assets and liabilities, details about your net worth, and so on. Write down your tentative financial goals. Now you can begin your budget plan.

Using Moneysanity

The freedom you have developed will enhance your life as you apply what you have learned to practical situations. Your increased assertiveness and self-awareness will help you approach monetary experiences with greater confidence.

Always remember to distinguish neurotic ("money as tormentor") from non-neurotic ("money as mentor") money behavior. A drive for financial success and dreams of acquiring a vast sum of money, for example, can be healthy as long as you are aware of your financial goals and are comfortable and at peace with them. You should also ensure that they are not harmful to others, that they serve beneficent aims rather than self-destructive ones, and that they further healthy needs, not abusive ones. The object is to enjoy your money without anxiety or irrational self-denial, guilt, or insecurities.

Since all our money-related behavior has an emotional component, how we set up a budget, how we spend money, how we shop, how we use credit, how we handle loan applications, and how we pay our taxes—in short, the whole realm of our monetary actions—all involve an integration of our psychological and financial styles. When we dovetail these two aspects of our selves, then we truly achieve Moneysanity.

Building Your Strengths

Remember that as you strengthen the psychological side you must also build up the pragmatic side. Read financial books and the money-advice sections of newspapers and popular magazines, as well as the traditional financial journals like *Barrons*, *Fortune*, the *Financial Times*, and the *Wall Street Journal*. You can supplement your reading with educational programs at your local schools or on television. For information about qualified financial planners, refer to the International Association for Financial Planning in Atlanta, Georgia (they issue a Registry of Financial Planning Practitioners) or the Canadian Association of Financial Planners in Toronto, Ontario.

By increasing your knowledge and enhancing your self-awareness, you will be more free to make money, to manage it more usefully, and to be liberated from it psychologically. Your greater awareness of your style with monetary resources and the tendencies that go with it will place you in a position to make sound fiscal decisions. You can channel your pecuniary energies more powerfully and make conscious choices as to whether to pursue or avoid various courses of action.

Financial success is as much a function of psychological self-insight as it is of anything else. A healthy relationship with your money will allow you to turn your ideas confidently and securely into sound financial actions.

Conclusion

Money, in one form or another, will never go out of fashion. Certainly, the potential for conflicts and the extraordinary behavior that surrounds it will always be there too. People will still stay "attached" to other people by continuing to owe them money; they will still "marry money"; they will continue to "buy" love; they will choose spouses with limited finances to prove to themselves that they don't care about wealth; they will drop friends who do not have as much money as they do; they will be subject to all the money ills that flesh is heir to—in short, life will go on very much as it always has. With one major exception—the advent of Moneysanity.

Mind Over Money assumes that we can do something constructive to alleviate or remove our psychological hangups about money. We should not be in the dark about matters pertaining to one of our most fundamental activities—dealing with money.

Now that you have the basic fiscal and psychological advice you need, you should be able to run your monetary life with increased effectiveness. Your behavior around money is critical to your well-being. Give it the consideration and respect it deserves. Remember, it's a case of mind over money.

To the Readers of *Mind Over Money*

If you have any anecdotes and experiences regarding money that you would like to share with me, or if you wish to receive a brochure outlining Mind Over Money programs and related information, please write to me c/o Doubleday Canada Ltd., 105 Bond Street, Toronto, Ontario, M5B 1Y3, Canada.

Suggested Reading

The Psychology of Money

Béland, Paul, and Cronin, Isaac. *Money: Myths and Realities.* New York: Carroll and Graf Publishers, Inc., 1986.

Bernstein, Jacob. *The Investor's Quotient: The Psychology of Successful Investing in Commodities and Stocks.* New York: John Wiley, 1980.

Bergler, Edmund. *Money and Emotional Conflicts.* New York: International Universities Press, Inc., 1970.

Blotnick, Srully. *Winning: The Psychology of Successful Investing.* New York: McGraw-Hill, 1979.

Frank, Robert H. *Choosing the Right Pond: Human Behavior and the Quest for Status.* New York: Oxford University Press, 1985.

Goldberg, Herb, and Lewis, Robert. *Money Madness: The Psychology of Saving, Spending, Loving and Hating Money.* New York: New American Library, 1979.

Knight, James A. *For the Love of Money.* Philadelphia: J.B. Lippincott Company, 1968.

Lindgren, Henry Clay. *Great Expectations: The Psychology of Money.* Los Altos: William Kaufmann, Inc., 1980.

Maital, Shlomo. *Minds, Markets and Money: Psychological Foundations of Economic Behavior.* New York: Basic Books, 1982.

Weinstein, Bob. *Money Hang-Ups.* New York: John Wiley and Sons, Inc., 1982.

Wiseman, Thomas. *The Money Motive: A Study of an Obsession.* London: Hutchinson and Company, 1974.

Financial Life Planning

Anderson, Brian E. and Snyder, J. Christopher. *It's Your Money*. Toronto: Methuen, 1986.

Ashley, Paul P. *You and Your Will: The Planning and Management of Your Estate*. New York: New American Library, 1985.

Berg, Adrianne G. *Your Wealth Building Years*. New York: Newmarket Press, 1986.

King, Sydney, and Levy, Joseph. *It's Never Too Early: A Guide to Planning and Enjoying Your Retirement Lifestyle*. Toronto: Stoddart, 1985.

Loeb, Marshall. *1986 Money Guide*. Toronto: Little, Brown and Company, 1985.

Longhurst, Patrick, and Earle, Rose Marie. *Looking After the Future: An Up-to-date Guide to Pension Planning in Canada*. Toronto: Doubleday, 1987.

MacInnis, Lyman. *Get Smart! Make Your Money Count*. Scarborough, Ontario: Prentice-Hall Canada, Inc., 1983.

Meyer, Martin J. *Don't Bank on It!: How to Make up to 22% or More on Your Savings—All Fully Insured*. New York: Pocket Books, 1980.

Rogers, Mary, and Joyce, Nancy. *Women and Money*. New York: Avon Books, 1979.

Rosefsky, Bob. *Money Talks*. New York: John Wiley and Sons, 1985.

Stein, Benjamin J. *Financial Passages*. New York: Doubleday and Company, Inc., 1985.

Children and Money

Berg, Adrianne G. *Your Kids, Your Money: A Financial Survival Manual for Parents*. New Jersey: Prentice-Hall, Inc., 1985.

Davis, Ken, and Taylor, Tom. *Kids and Cash*. New York: Bantam Books, 1981.

Snyder, J. Christopher. *How to Teach Your Children about Money*. Toronto: Macmillan of Canada, 1982.

Weinstein, Grace W. *Children and Money: A Parent's Guide*. New York: New American Library, 1985.

Index

Affirmations, 28, 101-2
Allen, Woody, 140-41
Assertive Behavior Training, 81-85
Assertiveness, life insurance and, 141-43
Attitudes, negative money, 64-66

Banks, borrowing money from, 207-9
Bargain hunter (*see also* "Bargainer, Sarah"), 43-50; as combination of spendthrift and miser, 46; development of, 6, 47-48; Moneyanalysis Quiz, 43-45; Moneysanity Evaluation Chart, 50; symptoms, 46, 49; treatment, 48-49
"Bargainer, Sarah" (*see also* Bargain hunter), 46-49, 141, 163
Behavior, eliminating or downplaying positive, 65
Benchley, Robert, 118
Bergler, Dr. Edmund, 29
Blame. *See* Letting Go
Blotnick, Srully, 117
Books. *See* Publications, financial
Borrowing money 203-19; from banks, 207-9; "borrow-phobia," 205-13; Green Therapies, 214-15; preparations for, 215-16; psychological difficulties about, 203-13; tips on, 216-19
Budgets, 109-24; "budgetitis," 116-18; establishing priorities for, 110, 112-16; how to create, 118-24; 238; importance of, 109-12; Money-Value Analysis Quiz, 114-15; 120

Children: and money, 134-37, 237; firstborn, as spendthrifts, 31

Cognitive Behavior Therapy, 63-70, 71
Commands, excessive use of, 65-66
Compulsive saver, 125-27, 130
Compulsive shopper. *See* Spendthrift
Compulsive under-saver, 126, 128-29
Computer buying services, 30
Conclusions, arbitrary, 64-65
Conclusions, jumping to, 66
Courses, financial, 4, 239
Creating Your Own Dictionary, 105-6
Credit, psychological difficulties with, 193-97
Credit cards, 193-202; Green Therapies, 198-99; how to use, 199-202; pros and cons of, 202; and spendthrifts, 196-97; tips about, 200-201
Credit rating, establishing, 199-200

Darvi, Bella, 56
Death, fear of: and life insurance, 140-41, 143-44; and writing a will, 152-54
Death, spendthrift's denial of, 31
Debts. *See* Borrowing money; Credit cards
Destressing. *See* Systematic Relaxation
Dictionary, Creating Your Own, 105-6
Dostoyevski, Fyodor, 56-57

Education, financial. *See* Courses, financial
Eliminating or downplaying positive behavior, 65
Emotional baggage, 92-93
Equations of money, 5-7

Estate: for life insurance, 148; terminology, 159; and writing a will, 156-57
Executor of will, 159-60

Fields, C.W., 20
Financial personality, 175-77, 182-88
Financial planning associations, 239
Forgiveness. *See* Letting Go
Franklin, Benjamin, 125, 166

"Gamble, Larry" (*see also* Gambler), 54-56, 71-72, 196-97
Gambler (*see also* "Gamble, Larry"), 51-59; Moneyanalysis Quiz, 51-53; Moneysanity Evaluation Chart, 58-59; symptoms, 54-55, 57; treatment, 55-56, 58-59
Getty, J.P., 20, 136
Green Therapies, definition of, 61-62
Green Therapies, suggested; for bargain hunter, 48, 50; for gambler, 56, 58-59; for miser, 18-19, 22; for spendthrift, 28, 33; for tycoon, 42
Green Therapies, suggested, for difficulties with: borrowing money, 214-15; budgets, 117-18; credit cards, 198-99; investments, 179-81; life insurance, 146-47; retirement, 226-27; saving money, 132; taxes, 168; writing a will, 155-56
Guided Imagery, 102-3

Hunt, L.L., 20

Insurance, borrowing money and, 218
Insurance, life. *See* Life insurance
Interest, compound, 134, 137
Investments, 172-92; borrowing money for, 218-19; and financial personality, 175-77, 182-88; preparations for making, 181-82, 184-89; psychological difficulties with, 172-74, 177-81; tips about making, 189-92

Knight, James, 7, 135
Knowledge, financial, importance of, 239-40
Kresge, S.S., 20
Kübler-Ross, Elisabeth, 143

Labelings, faulty, 65
Leacock, Stephen, 208
Le Carré, John, 197
Letting Go, 92-96
Life insurance, 140-51; and assertiveness, 141-43; attitudes to, 140-41; 143-45; Green Therapies, 146-47; how much you need, 148-49; and inflation, 150; kinds of, 149; psychological difficulties with, 145-46; tips for buying, 147-52; value of estate, 148
Lindgren, Henry, 207, 213
Loans. *See* Borrowing money
Looking-Forward Calendar, 103
Love, money and, 5-6, 27-28, 194

Magazines. *See* Publications, financial
Maugham, W. Somerset, 144
Meyer, Martin, 207
Miser (*see also* "Tightwad, Gerald"), 12-22; combined with spendthrift as bargain hunter, 46; Moneyanalysis Quiz, 12-15; Moneysanity Evaluation Chart, 22; symptoms, 17, 20-21; treatment, 18-19, 22
Money: children and, 134-37, 237; defined, 1-3; loss of, 7-9; love and, 5-6, 27-28, 194; management program, 236-38; obsession with (*see* Tycoon); personal philosophy of, 236
Money neurosis, 1-9
Money psychohistory, 76-78

Index

Money, equations of, 5-7
Moneyanalysis Quizzes, x, 61; for bargain hunter, 43-45; for gambler, 51-53; for miser, 12-15; for spendthrift, 23-26; for tycoon, 34-36
Moneysanity, 234-40; benefits of, 234-36; defined, 4-5; and needs, 78; personal philosophy of money, 236; test, 9-10; using, 238-40
Moneysanity evaluation, purpose of, 61
Moneysanity Evaluation Charts: for bargain hunter, 50; for gambler, 58-59; for miser, 22; for spendthrift, 33; for tycoon, 42
Money-Value Analysis Quiz, 114-15, 120
Morris, Arthur, the Morris Plan and, 215

Nash, Ogden, 125
Negative money attitudes, 64-66
Neurosis, money, 1-9

Obsession with money. *See* Tycoon
Overgeneralizations, 64-65
Overpersonalizing, 65
Overspending. *See* Spendthrift

Perception, negative selective, 65
Personality, financial, 175-77, 182-88
Phillippi, Dr. Grover, 178
Photograph Identification, 103-4
Progressive Relaxation. *See* Systematic Relaxation
Psychodynamics, 76-80
Psychohistory, money, 76-78
Psychological Flashcards, 86-91
Publications, financial, 4, 239

Relaxation. *See* Systematic Relaxation
Reston, James, 125

Retirement, 220-31; expenses after, 228; and financial fears, 220-25; financial planning for, 227-28; meaning of, 223; and savings, 134; sources of income after, 228, 230; and taxes, 230; tips on, 228-31
Role playing, 83-84, 104-5
Rothschild, Nathan, 19-20

Saver, compulsive, 125-27, 130
Saving money, 125-39; compound interest, 134, 137; compulsive saver, 125-27, 130; compulsive under-saver, 126, 128-29; and personal history, 130-31; plans for, 133-34; and retirement, 134; teaching children about, 134-35; tips for, 137-39
Shopaholics, 27
Shopper, compulsive. *See* Spendthrift
Spendermenders, 27, 30-31
Spendthrift (*see also* "Spendthrift, Joyce"), 23-33; combined with miser as bargain hunter, 46; and credit cards, 196-97; development of, 6, 29, 31; Moneyanalysis Quiz, 23-26; Moneysanity Evaluation Chart, 33, Shopaholics, 27; Spendermenders, 27, 30-31; symptoms, 31-32; treatment, 28, 30-31, 33
"Spendthrift, Joyce" (*see also* Spendthrift), 27-29, 82
Spooner, John, 177-78
Stein, Benjamin, 133-34
Stinginess, *See* Miser
Systematic Relaxation, 18, 71-75; for bargain hunter, 48; for gambler, 71-72; for miser, 18; for spendthrift, 28

Taxes, 162-71; and bargain hunter, 163; and borrowing money, 218; evading, 166-67; psychological difficulties with, 162-68; and retirement, 230; tips about, 169-71; and tycoon, 163

Television home-buying, 30
Tell-a-Tape, 105
Thinking, black or white, 64-65
Thought Stopping, 97-100
Thoughts, automatic, 66-69
"Tightwad, Gerald" (see also Miser), 16-19, 64, 126, 141
Trusts, writing a will and, 157-58
Tycoon (see also "Tycoon, Richard"), 34-42; Moneyanalysis Quiz, 34-36; Moneysanity Evaluation Chart, 42; development of, 38; symptoms, 40-41; treatment, 38-39, 42
"Tycoon, Richard" (see also Tycoon), 37-39, 163

"Underground economy," taxes and, 166-67

Under-saver, compulsive, 126, 128-29

Will, writing a, 152-61; and estate planning, 156-57; executor, 159-60; and fear of death, 152-54; Green Therapies, 155-56; procrastination, 152, 154; terminology, 159; tips for, 158-61; and trusts, 157-58
Williams, Tennessee, 31, 220
Wiseman, Thomas, 37
Women, credit rating and, 199

Zanuck, Darryl F., 56